Remember This

Remember This

Fresh Page Ideas
to Scrapbook the Year

**Kimber McGray
& Summer Fullerton**

MEMORY
MAKERS
BOOKS

Cincinnati, Ohio

Remember This. Copyright © 2010 by Kimber McGray and Summer Fullerton. Manufactured in China. All rights reserved. It is permissible for the purchaser to make the projects contained herein and sell them at fairs, bazaars and craft shows. No other part of this book may be reproduced in any form or by any electronic or mechanical means including information storage and retrieval systems without permission in writing from the publisher, except by a reviewer, who may quote a brief passage in review. Published by Memory Makers Books, an imprint of F+W Media, Inc., 4700 East Galbraith Road, Cincinnati, Ohio 45236. (800) 289-0963. First edition.

14 13 12 11 10   5 4 3 2 1

Distributed in Canada by Fraser Direct
100 Armstrong Avenue
Georgetown, ON, Canada L7G 5S4
Tel: (905) 877-4411

Distributed in the U.K. and Europe by David & Charles
Brunel House, Newton Abbot, Devon, TQ12 4PU,
England
Tel: (+44) 1626 323200, Fax: (+44) 1626 323319
E-mail: postmaster@davidandcharles.co.uk

Distributed in Australia by Capricorn Link
P.O. Box 704, S. Windsor, NSW 2756 Australia
Tel: (02) 4577-3555

Library of Congress Cataloging-in-Publication Data

McGray, Kimber.
  Remember this / Kimber McGray and Summer Fullerton.
       p. cm.
  Includes bibliographical references and index.
  ISBN-13: 978-1-59963-091-5 (pbk. : alk. paper)
  ISBN-10: 1-59963-091-5 (pbk. : alk. paper)
1. Photograph albums. 2. Photographs--Conservation and restoration. 3. Scrapbooking. I. Fullerton, Summer, II. Title.
  TR501.M4187 2010
  745.593--dc22
                    2009039939

fw media
www.fwmedia.com

EDITOR:
Kristin Boys

DESIGNER:
Geoffrey Raker

COVER DESIGN:
Rachael Smith

PRODUCTION COORDINATOR:
Greg Nock

PHOTOGRAPHERS:
Al Parrish, Ric Deliantoni

STYLIST:
Nora Martini

Metric Conversion Chart

to convert	to	multiply by
Inches	Centimeters	2.54
Centimeters	Inches	0.4
Feet	Centimeters	30.5
Centimeters	Feet	0.03
Yards	Meters	0.9
Meters	Yards	1.1
Sq. Inches	Sq. Centimeters	6.45
Sq. Centimeters	Sq. Inches	0.16
Sq. Feet	Sq. Meters	0.09
Sq. Meters	Sq. Feet	10.8
Sq. Yards	Sq. Meters	0.8
Sq. Meters	Sq. Yards	1.2
Pounds	Kilograms	0.45
Kilograms	Pounds	2.2
Ounces	Grams	28.3
Grams	Ounces	0.035

Acknowledgments

Pulling this book together was a long process that couldn't have been done without the help of many different people.

First, we would like to thank our families who supported and encouraged us through this process. Thank you for enduring frozen pizza night more than once over the last year. Without your love and support, this book wouldn't have been possible.

To all the contributors who shared their beautiful pieces of art. Thank you for generously sharing with us the many ways in which we can capture the moments that we celebrate year after year. We are honored to have included your work in our book.

Finally, to the amazing people at F+W Media who put this book together. To Christine Doyle, who patiently listened to our many ideas and allowed us to create this book. To Kristin Boys, for your incredible ease to work with and kindness that made this process so enjoyable.

Contents

Chapter 1

Get fresh ideas for recording budding blooms, Mother's Day, Easter, birthdays and other special events that spring to life.

Chapter 2

Family vacations, summer camp, Fourth of July—here's the inspiration you need to scrap all that fun in the sun.

Chapter 3

Fall 69

Go back to school, watch falling leaves and celebrate Thanksgiving on a page with great reasons to "fall" in love with scrapping.

Chapter 4

Winter........89

Check out new ways to document those cozy, snow-filled days like Christmas, Valentine's Day, ski trips and more.

Introduction

DO YOU BELIEVE IN FATE? WE DO.

Several years ago, an acquaintance was pulling Summer through a bustling convention center in Anaheim, California. It was there she met fate, also known as Kimber.

Shortly after our very brief meeting we were both named to the 2007 Creating Keepsakes Hall of Fame; from there our friendship began. Over the years, we have become each other's sounding boards. We share ideas, ask opinions, celebrate successes and listen to frustrations. And we noticed a common thread: we are both traditional scrapbookers who tend to scrapbook the same events and topics year after year.

One of our goals in writing this book is to show you fresh ways to approach scrapbooking everyday life events that you scrap from year to year. Ultimately, we want to give you a book that will be a wonderful resource, a book that won't sit and collect dust, one you can return to throughout the year. *Remember This* is broken down by season, beginning in spring and taking you all the way through winter. The pages are filled with tons of inspiration, including 120 layouts, technique instruction, sketches and checklists to help you scrapbook all year long.

Notes:

1. to most of us, they're just weeds, but to three year
2. old girls, they are the most fantastic
3. part of springtime. these tiny white
4. flowers are <u>LOVED</u>
5. they're collected and counted & given to
6. their mothers. they become bracelets & crowns, necklaces & crowns.
7. kids will pop off the tops, and watch
8. them fly. seeing Addie play with
9. them reminds me of my own happy
10. childhood. gotta love it.

Those springtime FLOWERS

Chapter 1

Spring

Spring is a time for new beginnings. Many of us find ourselves emerging from the fog of a winter, shut in with our cameras in hand, ready to get outside. Spring is the time to take advantage of that motivation and begin a new scrapbooking journey through the year. So many of the layouts our contributors shared with us convey that feeling of a fresh start. Take your cues from our designers, dig into your supplies and pull out something bright and new! In this chapter, we will explore the many elements of spring from holidays, like St. Patrick's Day and Easter, to the first blooms and so much more.

Add an oversized accent

Julie created a uniquely wonderful layout about her daughter's fifth birthday. She took her layout from typical to special by adding a giant "5" to highlight her daughter's age. Then Julie added hand journaling around the giant number accent. When approaching your next birthday layout try Julie's fresh approach by adding an oversized accent complemented by whimsical journaling and fun photos.

by Julie Detlef

Supplies: Cardstock; patterned paper (Piggy Tales); alphas (Making Memories, Glitz); brads (Paper Studio); stamps (Glitz); ribbon (May Arts)

Spring Scrapping Checklist

- ☐ St. Patrick's Day
- ☐ March Madness
- ☐ Spring break
- ☐ Easter or Passover activities and celebrations
- ☐ Cinco de Mayo
- ☐ Mother's Day
- ☐ Memorial Day
- ☐ A day at the park
- ☐ First blooms of the season
- ☐ Gardening
- ☐ Outdoor parties
- ☐ Prom
- ☐ Spring cleaning
- ☐ Spring sports such as baseball/ softball, lacrosse and track
- ☐ Trip to the farmer's market

Stage a birthday shoot

Sometimes, as our children grow into their teens, we scrapbook fewer of their activities. Ronda has captured the forgotten teen years perfectly on this layout. Her journaling tells about a fabulous birthday, but this layout wouldn't have been complete without a backyard photo shoot. Try a fun photo shoot with your teens and their friends for their next birthday. You will not only have a cherished keepsake but also a different way to scrapbook yet another birthday.

by Ronda Palazzari

Supplies: Brushes by Anna Aspens and Katie Pertiet (Designer Digitals); buttons, frames by Katie Pertiet (Designer Digitals); patterned papers, jewels by Dreaming with Pixels (Cocoa Daisy); stitches by Katie Pertiet (Designer Digitals, Shabby Princess); Misc: journaling spots

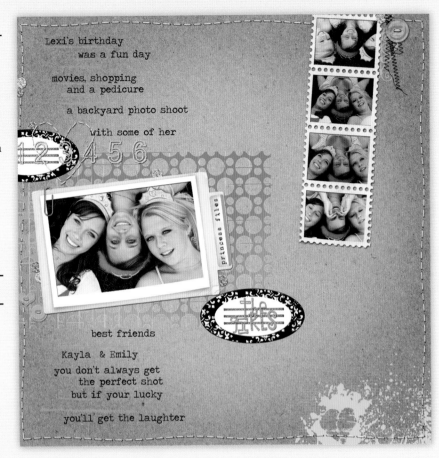

Document milestone birthdays

Milestones provide a built-in special theme for a birthday layout, even when using typical birthday accents. Kimber snapped these photos of her husband blowing out the candles on his 40th birthday cake. Note the simple birthday touches added to this layout, like premade chipboard accents. Also note how replacing the "i" in the title with a birthday candle instantly gives this layout a special birthday feel.

by Kimber McGray

Supplies: Cardstock; patterned paper (We R Memory Keepers); die-cut, alphas (Doodlebug Designs); stickers, brads (Making Memories); Misc: metal rimmed office tag

snow angel
gloves
dress for snow

march 2008
· the boys had
never seen SO
much SNOW!
They played
outside every
minute they could!

late march **BLIZZARD**

Get help from Mother Nature

When you're looking to create a unique page, sometimes Mother Nature helps you out! A springtime blizzard blanketed Laina's home with more snow than she could imagine, and she created this colorful layout to remember the experience. Spring layouts don't typically feature snow, so the photos automatically make for a different page. Plus, snow layouts don't usually boast primary color schemes, so this layout offers a refreshing twist.

by Laina Lamb

Supplies: Patterned paper (Cosmo Cricket, KI Memories); ribbon (KI Memories, Creative Imaginations); acrylic (Heidi Swapp); journaling block (Elle's Studio); rub-ons (Doodlebug Designs); alphas (American Crafts); chipboard (KI Memories); stickers (Making Memories, KI Memories, Cloud 9); brads (Making Memories)

Cleverly crop your photos

Katrina Kennedy spent St. Patrick's Day at a parade with her son. Long photo strips give the perfect glimpse of the parade, and the unexpected cropping provides a twist to a typical theme. The kraft color background is a simple backdrop that makes the stunning photos stand out.

by Katrina Kennedy

Supplies: Papers, brush by Katie Pertiet and Anna Aspnes (Designer Digitals); staple by Pattie Knox (Designer Digitals)

Happy St. Patrick's Day

There you sat. Thrilled. Entranced. Amazed. So many things to see. So much to take in. So many colors and shapes and sounds. Not quite certain what it was all about. But certain to talk about it for days after. Thrilled that it ended with a fire truck.

Embrace the theme

by Kimber McGray

Supplies: Cardstock (Core'dinations); patterned paper, die-cuts, ribbon (Jillibean Soup); die-cut alphas/numbers (QuicKutz); Misc: punches

Sometimes, the expected is just what you need for a fabulous page. Using fun green patterned paper and a simple homemade shamrock highlights the theme of this St. Patrick's Day page. You can create your own simple shamrock using a small heart punch. Punch hearts from cardstock or patterned paper and gently fold each heart in half. Attach each to your layout, overlapping them to form a shamrock. Take a cue from Kimber and dust off your stash of forgotten punches. Getting creative with the basics will help you breathe new life into your layouts.

Craft a creative background

Don't forget about sports as a way to record the season. Angela took her daughter and a friend to their first professional basketball game and used photos and memorabilia from that day as the foundation for this layout. Angela punched holes in a random scallop pattern to mimic the look of a ball bouncing, creating an airy eyelet style for the page.

by Angela Urbano

Supplies: Cardstock; patterned paper (Scrappin' Sports); alphas, stickers (American Crafts); rub-ons (BasicGrey, KI Memories, 7Gypsies); Misc: ticket stubs, punch

Punch an Eyelet Background

WHAT YOU'LL NEED

pencil, anywhere hole punch, white eraser

1 Use a pencil to draw your design freehand.

2 Punch holes about every ½" (1cm) along the pencil lines. Erase any leftover pencil marks with a white eraser.

Record unique family traditions

Seder is a feast celebrating the Jewish holiday of Passover. We love Vivian's layout about how her family celebrates this Jewish holiday with a twist. Taking close-up photos to show unique details reinforces how the holiday is a little different at Vivian's house. Remember to follow Vivian's lead when you scrapbook your next special holiday layout, and record those unique memories that make your family special.

by Vivian Masket

Supplies: Cardstock; transparency (Hambly); chipboard (American Crafts); Misc: staples

{non-traditional}

SEDER

It starts with the ceremonial seder plate. There's flat-leaf parsley instead of regular (the foodie in me coming out!), the stuffed lamb instead of the lamb shank bone (I can't stand the smell of lamb cooking), and then there's the orange (which represents the need for gender equality). Then there's the Haggadah, the booklet read throughout the dinner. Seth wrote his own version and updates it every year, making sure to include humor and relevant political and pop culture references. (Charlton Heston and Neil Diamond always make appearances in the pages of our Haggadah.) About the only thing that's traditional is that I make at least two times more food than we need!

just having fun

Props. There are always props at our Passover celebrations. Susan has bags of Plague puppets, Four Questions puppets (don't ask), and a cardboard pyramid full of plastic frogs, bugs, dark glasses and so forth. I bought these masks at the Temple Sinai gift shop one year, and I think they were the best props yet. You can't eat dinner wearing them, of course, and you certainly can't read the Haggadah with them on, but they were fun nonetheless. Since this seder was held at my house, with its limited seating, there are only photos of seven plagues; not sure what happened to Beasts, Frogs & Cattle Disease, but it's clear who Sophie takes after--check out the upside-down masks on her & on Grandma!

'07

GOOD MEMORIES

passover props

Tell the story

Vivian's layout above tells a lighthearted and whimsical story of how masks played a role in Passover dinner in 2007. The colorful photos are well balanced by the use of light brown. Adding striped patterned paper in opposite quadrants of the layout draws your eye right to the photos. Bored with scrapping the same holiday year after year? Pick one tradition and tell the story in detail.

by Vivian Masket

Supplies: Cardstock; patterned paper (KI Memories, Scenic Route); overlay (Hambly); alphas (American Crafts); rub-ons (October Afternoon); Misc: punch

Photos by Mary Kay Seckinger

AIDEN WAS READY THIS YEAR. HE KNEW EXACTLY WHAT TO DO AND COULDN'T WAIT FOR MS. ELIZABETH TO OPEN THE FRONT DOOR! SO OFF HE WENT COLLECTING AS MANY EGGS AS HIS LITTLE BUCKET COULD HOLD. THEN IT BECAME A CHALLENGE TO KEEP HIM FROM OPENING THEM ALL UP. BUT WE DISTRACTED HIM WITH ART PROJECTS AND EGG COOKIES. ON THE WAY HOME HE STARTED OPENING THEM AND WAS SO SURPRISED TO SEE THE GOODIES INSIDE. EASTER 2008

ready.set hunt

Create a photo time line

Every year Easter provides a variety of activities to scrapbook. Lisa captured the simplicity of an Easter egg hunt in this layout. On your next holiday layout, line up your photos to create a time line of events. Combine this with detailed journaling and your layout will be uniquely complete. Lisa used three photos to achieve this look, but you can take this idea farther by using more photos and spreading them over two pages.

by Lisa Carroll

Supplies: Cardstock; patterned paper (Chatterbox, GCD Studios); chipboard (American Crafts, GCD Studios); stickers (Doodlebug Designs)

Make a mini album

Mini albums are a wonderful way to encompass the events of an entire day all in one place. Holidays, such as Easter, are packed full of many activities and can be traditionally scrapbooked over multiple pages. Try printing a select group of photos and creating a "favorites" mini album. Depending on the theme of your album, you can embellish it with all kinds of accents from brads, to rub-ons, to flowers. Mini albums can be tailored to fit any subject or theme and are a refreshing change from a traditional scrapbook layout.

by Anabelle O'Malley

Supplies: Chipboard, felt (Queen & Co.); jewels (Heidi Swapp); die-cut (KI Memories); patterned paper, rub-ons (Pink Paislee); ribbon (Michael's); stickers (Pink Paislee, Scenic Route)

we love to dye Easter eggs + we have plenty of supplies to use each year. Margret and I were into doing multicolor eggs this year, while Audrey really liked putting stickers on hers. we made a great batch

we add vinegar to the dyes.

Audrey takes her work very seriously!

the finished product

eGGS

Margret was really into dyeing this year.

2007

Take pre-holiday photos

When taking holiday photos, don't forget about activities leading up to the special day. In fact, pre-Easter egg-dying produces some of the most colorful photos—just look at Marci's layout. Brightly colored photos like these can be difficult to scrap. Try Marci's approach and use only strips of colorful patterned paper while leaving white space to balance out the busyness. Little bursts of color from patterned paper are all this layout needs. Highlight your journaling by attaching little tags as captions beneath the photos.

by Marci Lambert

Supplies: Cardstock; patterned paper (BasicGrey); brads, alphas (Making Memories); flowers (Prima); Misc: ink

Do Some Spring Cleaning

These days, most of us have traded boxes of photos for JPEG images on our computers. This spring, take your cleaning efforts from your closets to your computer. Take advantage of the tagging option offered in image-editing software like Adobe Photoshop Elements to organize your photos. You can also download free programs such as Picasa (http://picasa.google.com) to help with organization. If you don't have software on your computer, simply organize your photos into folders on your hard drive labeled by year, month and event. A little extra time spent today will make the scrapbooking process simpler all year long.

{when daddy was the}
white house
easter bunny

It was 1996, and your father was working in the Office of Presidential Letters and Messages at the White House. The opportunity arose for him to be one of the White House Easter bunnies and he jumped at the chance. He spent the morning posing for pictures, waving at and talking to kids, and hopping and dancing behind Al Roker as the "Today Show" covered the White House Easter Egg Roll. The highlight for your dad, however, occurred when a little boy named Jason handed him a package of carrots and said, "Easter Bunny, you're my best friend."

Scrap old holiday photos

Scrapbook layouts are a wonderful vehicle for telling those stories your family loves to hear over and over again. Vivian sent us this wonderfully unique layout featuring her husband as a White House Easter bunny. This layout documents a little piece of family history. Follow Vivian's lead and dig out those older photos and tell the stories you want your family to remember for a lifetime.

by Vivian Masket

Supplies: Cardstock; patterned paper, chipboard (American Crafts); digital element by Katie Pertiet (Designer Digitals)

Create movement

Summer's daughter came home from school with a container full of ladybugs and Summer snapped a few photos for this springtime layout. The close-up photos show her daughter's total fascination with her newfound friends. Take advantage of your camera's zoom lens and use close-up photos to show off a smaller subject. Then create movement for a lively layout using a trail of accents. In this layout Summer used flowers to enhance the spring feel. You can relate this idea to almost any themed layout by changing the accent.

by Summer Fullerton

Supplies: Cardstock; patterned paper, chipboard, eyelets, stickers (American Crafts); stamps (Ink Boutique); Misc: ink

Print wallet-sized photos

You just came home from a springtime outing and your memory card is full. How are you going to scrapbook all those photos? No problem! Leigh's two-page layout boasts 21 small photos. Not only can you scrap a full day on one two-page layout, you can save a little money, too. Many photo processors will print two wallet-sized photos on a 4" × 6" (10cm × 15cm) sheet without charging an additional fee. Wallet photos are also great options for scrapping smaller layout sizes and mini albums.

by Leigh Penner

Supplies: Cardstock; patterned paper, buttons (SEI); stamps (Autumn Leaves); Misc: ink

Journal around the page

A strong commitment to family, faith and community is wonderfully portrayed in Wendy's layout. The page combines many elements without looking overcrowded and cramped. By using a soft color palette, simple floral accents and a collection of small photos, this layout captures the special event perfectly. Wendy took a unique approach to her journaling by writing around the perimeter of the page. Take your layout to the next level with special journaling touches that go beyond the basic.

by Wendy Kwok

Supplies: Patterned paper, ribbon, stickers (Making Memories); stamps (October Afternoon); Misc: ink, punch

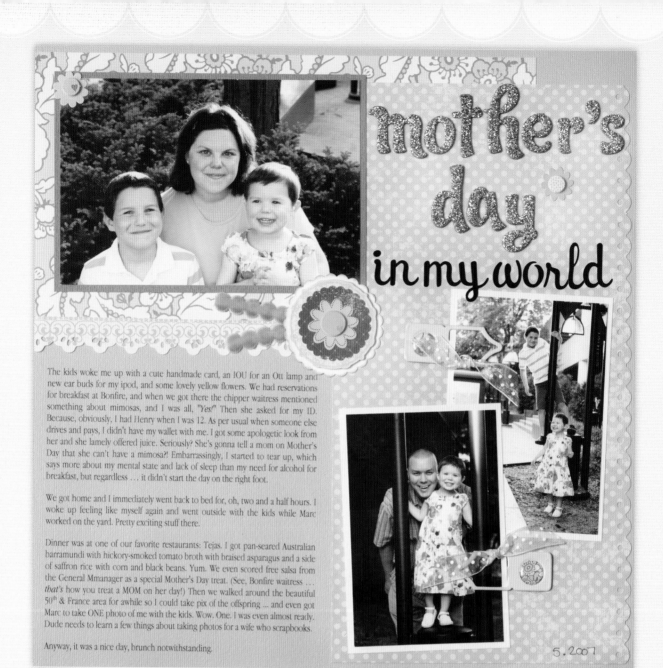

The kids woke me up with a cute handmade card, an IOU for an Ott lamp and new ear buds for my ipod, and some lovely yellow flowers. We had reservations for breakfast at Bonfire, and when we got there the chipper waitress mentioned something about mimosas, and I was all, *"Yes!"* Then she asked for my ID. Because, obviously, I had Henry when I was 12. As per usual when someone else drives and pays, I didn't have my wallet with me. I got some apologetic look from her and she lamely offered juice. Seriously? She's gonna tell a mom on Mother's Day that she can't have a mimosa?! Embarrassingly, I started to tear up, which says more about my mental state and lack of sleep than my need for alcohol for breakfast, but regardless … it didn't start the day on the right foot.

We got home and I immediately went back to bed for, oh, two and a half hours. I woke up feeling like myself again and went outside with the kids while Marc worked on the yard. Pretty exciting stuff there.

Dinner was at one of our favorite restaurants: Tejas. I got pan-seared Australian barramundi with hickory-smoked tomato broth with braised asparagus and a side of saffron rice with corn and black beans. Yum. We even scored free salsa from the General Mmanager as a special Mother's Day treat. (See, Bonfire waitress … *that's* how you treat a MOM on her day!) Then we walked around the beautiful 50th & France area for awhile so I could take pix of the offspring … and even got Marc to take ONE photo of me with the kids. Wow. One. I was even almost ready. Dude needs to learn a few things about taking photos for a wife who scrapbooks.

Anyway, it was a nice day, brunch notwithstanding.

Take time to journal

Michele created the ideal Mother's Day layout by combining beautiful product with straight-from-the-heart journaling. Her story of how she spent Mother's Day 2007 is brilliantly written with a touch of humor. Scrapbooks capture an event through photos, but your words fill it with emotion. Try Michele's approach and tell the complete story behind your holiday photos. Journaling can be one of the hardest parts of scrapbooking, but taking the extra time will make for more interesting holiday layouts and enhanced memories.

by Michele Skinner

Supplies: Cardstock; patterned paper (Autumn Leaves, Making Memories, Creative Imaginations); alphas (American Crafts); clips (Autumn Leaves); stickers (Heidi Grace, Creative Imaginations); ribbon (Offray, Making Memories); Misc: ink

FOR THE
RECORD

SUBJECT: Motherhood
DATE: 2008

It certainly hasn't been easy. Some days I doubt myself so so much. Sometimes I cry and pray for patience. But those two little girls own my heart. I can't believe I made them, that these beautiful babies came from me. It's not a perfect journey. But the smiles far out-weigh the tears. I've become a mama I'm proud of. But I'm still a total work in progress. I love being "mama."

Becoming
mama

Use it to reflect

The day you become a mother is the day your life changes forever. So why not take the time next Mother's Day to reflect on the journey? On this layout, Stephanie recalls her feelings about transitioning from a family of three to a family of four. Scrapping holidays doesn't require you to scrap the actual day. Using the event to prompt introspection is a great way to keep holiday pages fresh.

by Stephanie Howell

Supplies: Patterned paper (Narratives, October Afternoon, Autumn Leaves); journaling card (Collage Press); flowers (Prima); buttons (Autumn Leaves); chipboard (American Crafts); label (Two Girlz Stuff); alphas (American Crafts, Making Memories)

Take advantage of paper patterns

Embrace the seasonal weather, grab your camera and get outside! Angie did just this and captured a simple moment of her daughter picking a bouquet of springtime weeds. Spring layouts can be accented with scallops that give the illusion of flower petals. Take advantage of your patterned paper when looking to accent your layout. Angie cut along the pattern and was left with a unique scallop border that is the perfect accompaniment for a spring-themed page.

by Angie Hagist

Supplies: Patterned paper (October Afternoon, Scenic Route); stamps (October Afternoon); die-cuts (October Afternoon, SEI); metal letters (JoAnn's); ribbon (May Arts); Misc: ink

Show time-lapsed photos

Spring is a time of growth, and Emily's time-lapsed photos are a fresh take on scrapping springtime flowers. The photos of the blooming cherry trees are lovely and show how much things can change in a short period of time. When creating a similar layout, line your photos in a row and add the date under each one to create a time line.

by Emily Pitts

Supplies: Cardstock; frames, staples, string by Katie Pertiet (Designer Digitals); journaling spot by Sande Kreiger (Two Peas in a Bucket); metal tag by Shannon Freeman (Two Peas in a Bucket)

Use a monochromatic scheme

Prom is a rite of passage, so Andrea created this colorful tone-on-tone layout celebrating her niece's special dance. Using a monochromatic color scheme allowed Andrea to relate her photos, title and embellishments. Notice the array of photos taken in addition to the typical prom couple portrait. Andrea grabbed shots of details and action, and "coupled" with the color scheme, they make for a cheery page quite appropriate for a happy occasion.

by Andrea Amu

Supplies: Cardstock; patterned paper, chipboard, stamp (Fancy Pants); brad (Doodlebug); die-cut (QuickKutz); flowers (Creative Impressions); Misc: ink

Teach with a layout

When we share our scrapbooks with our friends we don't just inspire; we also teach. On this layout, Nic shares about Anzac Day, which is celebrated in Australia and New Zealand. Our layouts serve as so much more than pretty compilations of patterned paper and photos. They are tools to teach our children, friends and others about traditions, family, love, friendship and so much more. Take a cue from Nic and create your next layout with the intent to teach someone something about yourself.

by Nic Howard

Supplies: Cardstock; patterned paper (Teresa Collins, BasicGrey); alphas (American Crafts); die-cut (Making Memories); brads (BasicGrey); transparencies (Hambly, 7Gypsies); Misc: ink

Remember memorabilia

Be proud of your accomplishments, and scrapbook successes throughout the year. Emily participated in a 10k race in the spring of 2008, and this layout represents her accomplishment. Memorabilia like the bib from the race puts this layout ahead of the pack. To make seasonal layouts truly special, include memorabilia along with photos. Other items worth saving for layouts include ticket stubs, business cards, brochures and trip itineraries.

by Emily Pitts

Supplies: Cardstock; alphas (American Crafts); chipboard (Heidi Swapp, Scenic Route); ribbon (American Crafts)

It doesn't matter how much I claim I'm not a runner, the Bolder/Boulder 10K was just so exciting, I got caught up in, and away I went, finishing much faster than I ever did in my treadmill training. It's that way with every race, and I know I'll run next year too. May 26, 2008

BOLDER BOULDER
560
PF 560

i am not a runner

Enhance the title

How do your children spend their days after school? Do they play sports or participate in clubs? Laura Ping's son is a Boy Scout and he proudly participated in the annual Pinewood Derby. By using creative title work Laura ehanced the "race" theme behind this layout. You can achieve this same look using number stickers or patterned paper as the backdrop for your title

by Laura Ping

Supplies: Papers, binder clip by Gina Cabrera (Digital Design Essentials); letters (Purple Tulip Designs); tag (Katie Pertiet (Designer Digitals); brushes (Deviant Art); Misc: Cub Scout clip art, SchoolBully and Social Animal fonts

pinewood derby

after waiting all day for the paint on your car to dry. i completely ruined it when i tried to put the stickers on it. i ran to the hobby store, bought another car, painted it, assembled it, and put alien stickers on it. i was so worried you would be furious with me. you were actually really excited when you saw it. the day of the race you were proud to show it off -- even though it wasn't the car you made. your didn't come in first or win a trophy...you just had the time of your life. i was so proud of you. you have what it takes to be a great cub scout. keep it up! next year i will keep away from your car :)

APRIL 12TH, 2007
STONYCREEK ELEMENTARY

05
may 20
08

this was your first year of track. it was a learning experience for your team. but you excelled at the 55 meter race. Being first to reach the tape at the finish line was your goal a total victory and a meet to remember.

Victory

Repeat a focal photo

Individualize your next sports layout with roughed-up edges and grunge effects. Mary scrapbooked her son's first year of track by creating this dynamic digital layout. Try her unique approach to creating movement on a layout by layering the same photo multiple times. This layout is digital, but you could craft this same treatment by simply printing three copies of your focal photo and layering them on your layout.

by Mary Rogers

Supplies: White paper and stars by Lynn Grieveson (Designer Digitals); stitching holes, stamped trims, ledger grids, watery brushes and alphabet by Katie Pertiet (Designer Digitals); vertical date stamp by Kellie Mize (Designer Digitals); texture edge brushes by Anna Aspnes (Designer Digitals); Notebook font (Two Peas in a Bucket)

Arrange a digital collage

Do your children have a favorite outdoor activity? Sherry's son loves to skateboard. Using image-editing software, Sherry created a grungy photo collage showing off some favorite photos of her son skating. She printed the digital collage and used it as the base of this hybrid layout. Accents, like irregularly cut circles that mimic skateboard wheels and a playful title, enhance the skater theme. Try out some of Sherry's creative techniques on your next outdoor layout.

by Sherry Steveson

Supplies: Patterned paper, transparency, chipboard letters (Fancy Pants Designs); stamps (Hero Arts, Luxe Designs); puff paint (Tulip); Misc: ink

Whenever I see the abbreviation for Skate Spelled this way I think of the periodic table in chemistry. I bet Fletcher wishes his favorite pasttime was a formula he could just mix up.. or perhaps it is!

Turn a grid on an angle

Sports and warm weather go hand in hand, making for layout after layout of the same topic. Deena shows us how to take a sports layout to the next level. When faced with many photos, try Deena's graphic grid approach: Simply take a traditional grid and turn it on an angle. Let photos slide off the edges of your layout to create a modern look.

by Deena Wuest

Supplies: Purely Happy Paper by Katie Pertiet (Designer Digitals); Little Enamel Sports by Pattie Knox (Designer Digitals); Tortuga Template No. 25 by Kellie Mize (Designer Digitals); AllStar Brushes by Art Warehouse (Designer Digitals); Impact and Avant Garde fonts

The fourth of July in Yuma, AZ. We had such a great time. First we ate watermelon that was like eating candy. We played some games and then watched a really good demolition derby. The perfect ending to a great night was fireworks. What a great way to celebrate our Nation's Independence Day. God Bless America!

~July 4, 2008

4th of JULY

Chapter 2

Summer

As the mercury rises, we enjoy the brilliance of a hot summer day while our kids laugh and run through the sprinklers. (If you close your eyes, can you hear the laughter now?) If you're like us, then you take more photos during the summer months than other seasons. Family vacations, outdoor activities, fireworks displays and warm weather give us lots of reasons to snap photos. If your summer scrapping is beginning to get a bit dull, look no further than the ideas in this chapter—like Jennifer Lawrence's cork background on page 37 and Gina Fensterer's altered embellishment on page 54. Dive on into summer, and get inspired to dwindle down that stack of unscrapped photos.

Scan school papers

It's the end of the school year and you have amassed a large collection of artwork and papers from your child's year in school. Now what? A mini album is a fun alternative to traditional layouts and allows you to hold a year's worth of school memories in your hand. Scan children's artwork and shrink it down to fit on the mini pages. For an added bonus, include your child's handprint on the cover.

by Summer Fullerton

Supplies: Patterned paper (BasicGrey, Mustard Moon, Autumn Leaves); ribbon, buttons (Autumn Leaves); rub-ons (Heidi Grace, Jo-Ann); metal (BasicGrey); alphas (Heidi Swapp); flowers (Stavy Stamps); Misc: glitter, ink, staples, chipboard

The following text appears within the scrapbook layout image:

12345

Becca's 5th grade promotion was so wonderful. I can't even explain how proud I was when I watched her walk down that isle wearing her Presidents Award Medal around her neck while the graduation music played in the background. Becca not only graduated 5th grade with honors, but she was also involved in many school activities such as band, student council, and softball. She even earned the Citizenship Award earlier this year. All I can say is she is an awesome kid.

Make use of numbers

Whether it's moving on from kindergarten, going to middle school or just finishing a grade, school milestones should be celebrated. Take note of Sarah's use of numbers on this layout. They are the perfect embellishment to show off her daughter's promotion from fifth grade. Use your journaling to further expand upon a graduation layout by listing school accomplishments, awards and clubs.

by Sarah Mullanix

Supplies: Cardstock; patterned paper (Creative Imaginations, KI Memories, Making Memories, The Paper Studio); die-cuts (Provo Craft); flowers (K&Co.)

The Graduate

Derek Scott McElveen
Red Bank High School
Chattanooga, TN
May 18, 2008

Now he's 'Bama bound!!!

Add a dimensional title

Celebrate the graduate in your life with a simple layout. Sometimes less is more as Gretchen illustrates on this layout. Spice up a simple design with a dimensional title treatment layering a chipboard accent over letter stickers. School-themed rub-ons and stamps make perfect journaling blocks for graduation and other school pages.

by Gretchen McElveen

Supplies: Brads (Making Memories); chipboard (American Crafts, Heidi Swapp); patterned paper (BasicGrey, Scenic Route); rub-ons (Jenni Bowlin)

a GOOD day

So proud of these girls. Mother
and daughter—both starting
new chapters in their
lives. I'm so happy to
have been there to
witness all of it!

Provide texture with cork

Jennifer's layout is a wonderful glimpse into the life of a graduate—friends and family, happy memories, celebrating a great achievement. Subtle use of a clock stamp, grid paper, letters and ruled lines give this layout just the right school-themed touches. Plus, a cork background, reminiscent of a classroom, is a brilliant addition. It not only makes for a perfectly themed background, but also adds texture and dimension to the page.

by Jennifer Lawrence

Supplies: Cardstock; patterned paper (7Gypsies, October Afternoon, Fontwerks); cork (Contact); stamps (Heidi Swapp); stickers (Creative Imaginations, October Afternoon); felt (KI Memories); Misc: ink

Stitch your own accents

Summer's son has played baseball for several years and she has accumulated tons of photos. She took the traditional route in choosing themed product for this page, but she added a spin with interesting techniques. Summer created baseball accents with clear embossing powder and metal-rimmed tags. She also hand stitched around a single title letter and added additional stitching to accent the page.

by Summer Fullerton

Supplies: Cardstock; Brads (BasicGrey); chipboard, patterned paper, felt, stamp, stick pins (Inque Boutique); floss (DMC); embossing powder (Jo-Ann); tag (Making Memories); Misc: ink, punches

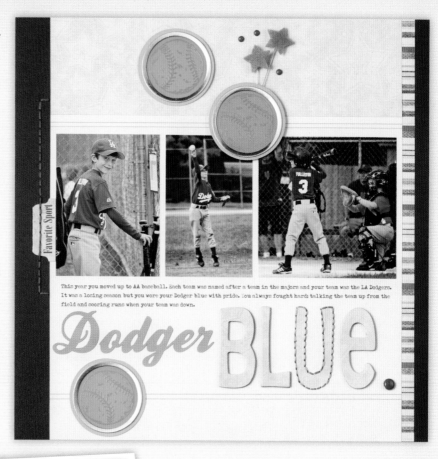

Fill in for a Missing Letter

WHAT YOU'LL NEED

chipboard letter negative, pencil, patterned paper or cardstock, micro-tip scissors, white eraser; optional: chalk ink, paint or pen

1

Set the negative chipboard piece on top of the patterned paper or cardstock. Trace around the inside of the negative with a pencil.

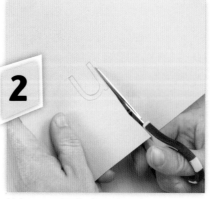

2

Using a pair of micro-tip scissors, cut around the pencil outline of the letter. When you are finished cutting out the letter, erase the pencil lines with a white eraser.

Variation

Set the chipboard negative directly onto your background. Apply chalk ink, paint or pen to fill in the letter.

He is an athlete. A competitor. He's done karate, soccer, baseball, football, track + field, swimming, biking, triathalons + tennis. All well. But tennis has won over his heart. He plays 3-4 times a week and boy does he play hard.

№ 480193

PLAY HARD

it doesn't get any better than this

date:

Capture the action

Don't forget your significant other when it comes to documenting summer activities. Angie created this clean and simple layout documenting one of the summer activities her husband loves—playing tennis. She kept her layout fun and youthful by using an orange background, journaling ticket stubs and glitter letter stickers. Capture the action just like Angie did by using the action mode on your camera. Just because we are all grown up doesn't mean we should give up playing like a kid, nor should we forget to scrap those activities.

by Angie Hagist

Supplies: Cardstock; patterned paper (October Afternoon, Sassafras Lass); alphas (October Afternoon, Making Memories); stickers (October Afternoon)

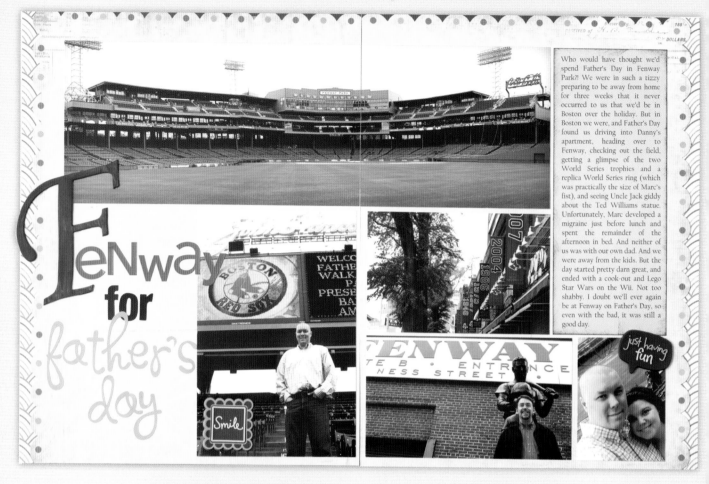

Fenway for father's day

Who would have thought we'd spend Father's Day in Fenway Park?! We were in such a tizzy preparing to be away from home for three weeks that it never occurred to us that we'd be in Boston over the holiday. But in Boston we were, and Father's Day found us driving into Danny's apartment, heading over to Fenway, checking out the field, getting a glimpse of the two World Series trophies and a replica World Series ring (which was practically the size of Marc's fist), and seeing Uncle Jack giddy about the Ted Williams statue. Unfortunately, Marc developed a migraine just before lunch and spent the remainder of the afternoon in bed. And neither of us was with our own dad. And we were away from the kids. But the day started pretty darn great, and ended with a cook-out and Lego Star Wars on the Wii. Not too shabby. I doubt we'll ever again be at Fenway on Father's Day, so even with the bad, it was still a good day.

Tell the whole story

Remember, photos often don't tell the entire story. Detailed journaling can pull a layout together and will keep layouts exciting and fresh. At first glance, Michele's layout appears to be about Father's Day at the ballpark. Pretty typical. But reading her journaling will tell you it wasn't the most traditional of days—her husband spent the day away from his children and ended up with a migraine. How did you spend Father's Day this year? Tell the story on a layout.

by Michele Skinner

Supplies: Cardstock; patterned paper (Scenic Route, Pink Paislee); alphas (Zsiage, Doodlebug, American Crafts); stickers (October Afternoon); Misc: ink

i spy

PHOTOS BY GRANT

PHOTO OP

ALWAYS EXPLORE

Grant received a video camera for Christmas this year. He quickly discovered he could take still photos as well as videos. He now takes more photos. These are just a few of his photos from our trip to Pacific City. Not bad for an 11 year old? ● June 2008

PHOTOS BY MOM

sand dunes ● the condo where we stayed ● a beach full of surfers ● a photo of your reflection ● Haystack Rock ●

Get a new perspective

Take a new approach to family vacations and turn your camera over to someone else. On a recent trip to the Oregon coast, Summer's son brought his video camera to take still shots. Using his photos, she was able to scrapbook the trip from his perspective. On your next trip, hand your children disposable cameras. Seeing your adventure from a new perspective will add a fresh twist to vacation pages.

by Summer Fullerton

Supplies: Cardstock; patterned paper (Scenic Route, Prima); chipboard accent (Scenic Route); alphas (Heidi Grace); die-cut (October Afternoon); brads (BasicGrey); stamp (Autumn Leaves); metal tag rim (Making Memories); label (Dymo); buttons (Foofala); Misc: ink

Go exotic

Don't put those one-of-a-kind photos on ordinary travel-themed paper. If you're visiting exotic lands this summer, then you better be ready to create an exotic layout to show off the photos! Emeline's wonderful use of product gives this layout a textured and tropical feel. You, too, can get tropical by using a blue and green color scheme. Clear accents and alphas enhance the effect by mimicking the look of water.

by Emeline Seet

Supplies: Cardstock; patterned paper (Rusty Pickle); alphas (Heidi Swapp, Li'l Davis); chipboard (Li'l Davis); overlay (Creative Imaginations); stickers (Creative Imaginations, Making Memories, KI Memories); rub-on (Scenic Route); tag (Making Memories); journaling card (Elle Studios); netting (Glitz Design); Misc: acrylic paint

Add architectural interest

Like any good scrapper, Paula took tons of scenic photos after given the opportunity to explore Ireland. To fit them all in one page she created a digital photo montage of local architecture from a day trip. Paula topped the montage with not-so-traditional travel-themed paper. If you're looking to make your next trip's album stand out from the rest, explore your surroundings and take photos of the local architecture in addition to the traditional sights.

by Paula Gilarde

Supplies: Patterned paper (Making Memories, BasicGrey); alphas (Scrapworks); stickers (Making Memories); button (KI Memories)

Use a cardstock background

If you're like most scrappers, your albums are littered with summer vacation layouts. Sarah sent us this layout that immediately caught our eye with a simple design that shows off the photos. Vacation pages tend to have a lot of photos showing a variety of subjects. Try Sarah's approach and pair busier photos with simple embellishments and cardstock. Using a wild patterned paper can distract from the photos, but a cardstock-only layout can make photos shine.

by Sarah Hough

Supplies: Cardstock; patterned paper (October Afternoon); rub-on, chipboard (KI Memories); alphas (Making Memories); buttons (Autumn Leaves)

Journal in a digital box

When Leigh created this hybrid layout, she went right for vacation-themed products to show off her photos. She made the design her own by adding a colored journaling box sandwiched between two photos. You can create a simple colored journaling box using your word-processing program. Just create a text box, fill it with color and type with white text. We love this idea because it can be customized to match any layout and layered under fun title letters for a creative page.

by Leigh Penner

Supplies: Patterned paper (Making Memories, My Mind's Eye); brads, chipboard (Making Memories); digital brush by Katie Pertiet (Designer Digitals)

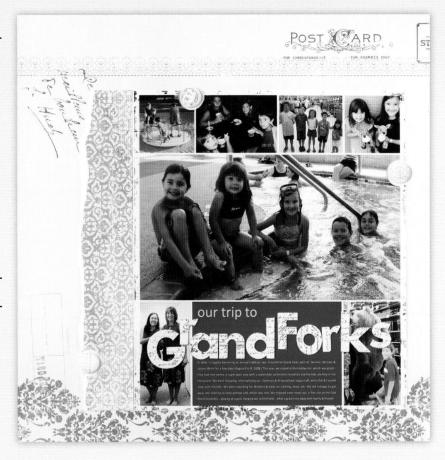

Summarize the trip

After the end of a fabulous vacation you probably find yourself overloaded with photos. Tracey created this title page for a Disney vacation album, but the idea works just as well for creating a single page for an entire trip. When faced with piles of pictures, make a summary page using a large variety of photos from your trip. Today many photo processors offer a variety of different sizes, so take advantage of the diverse selection to make a photo collage on your next layout.

by Tracey Locher

Supplies: Cardstock; patterned paper, chipboard, trim (Rusty Pickle); flowers (Prima, Making Memories); alphas (Adornit); rhinestones (Darice)

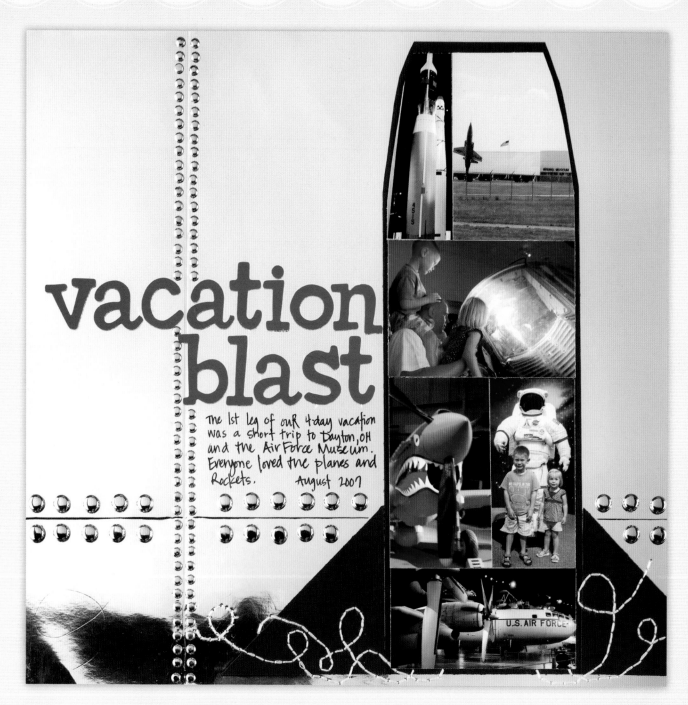

vacation blast

The 1st leg of ouR 4-day vacation was a short trip to Dayton, OH and the Air Force Museum. Everyone loved the planes and Rockets.   August 2007

Have a blast

If you're trying to find a unique way to scrap the same old summer vacation photos, then take a cue from Kimber and turn specialty paper into exactly what you need to show them off. This metallic paper was the perfect accompaniment to Kimber's Air Force museum photos. Kimber added brads to look like rivets, cropped photos in the shape of a rocket ship and added creative stitching to scrapbook these museum memories.

by Kimber McGray

Supplies: Cardstock; alphas (American Crafts); brads (Making Memories); thread (DMC)

Create a Rocket-Themed Layout

WHAT YOU'LL NEED

cardstock, wallet-sized photos, craft knife/scissors/paper trimmer, adhesive, bone folder, ruler, paper piercer or thumb tack, mat, brads, craft stick

1 Lay a wallet-sized photo on to a piece of black cardstock and trim along the edges to create a strip. This will be the base of the rocket.

2 Trim down other wallet-sized photos to fill in the base of the cardstock strip. Adhere the photos to the cardstock.

3 Trim the top of the rocket strip at an angle. You'll also need to trim the photos to fit. Then cut two triangles to fit at either side of the rocket's base.

4 To create the riveted metal effect, score two intersecting lines on the background.

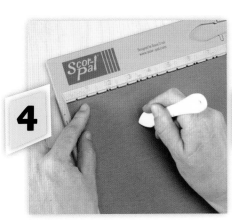

5 Using a ruler as a guide, pierce holes in the background on either side of the scored line. (Place a mat underneath the paper.) For larger brads, space holes about ½" (1 cm) apart. For smaller brads space holes about ¼" (6mm) apart.

6 Place brads in the holes. Opening many brads can be tiring on fingers, so use the paper piercer to open the prongs and a craft stick to flatten them.

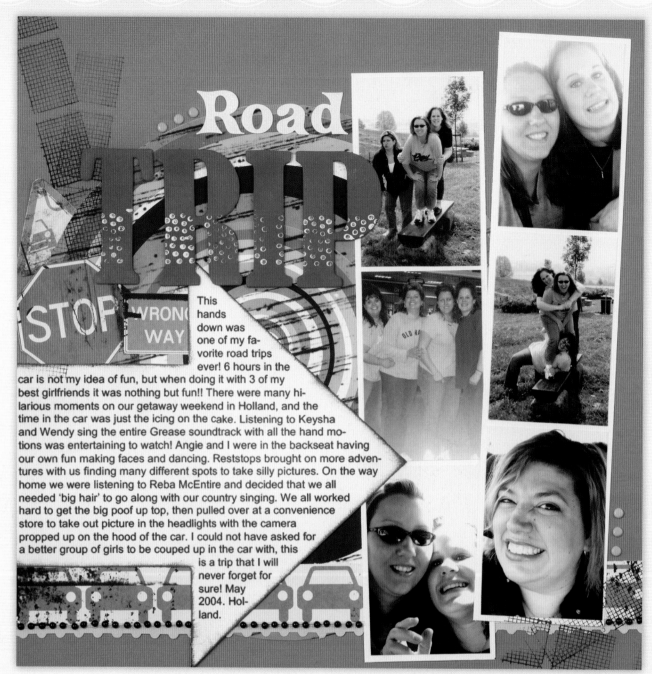

Road TRIP

This hands down was one of my favorite road trips ever! 6 hours in the car is not my idea of fun, but when doing it with 3 of my best girlfriends it was nothing but fun!! There were many hilarious moments on our getaway weekend in Holland, and the time in the car was just the icing on the cake. Listening to Keysha and Wendy sing the entire Grease soundtrack with all the hand motions was entertaining to watch! Angie and I were in the backseat having our own fun making faces and dancing. Reststops brought on more adventures with us finding many different spots to take silly pictures. On the way home we were listening to Reba McEntire and decided that we all needed 'big hair' to go along with our country singing. We all worked hard to get the big poof up top, then pulled over at a convenience store to take out picture in the headlights with the camera propped up on the hood of the car. I could not have asked for a better group of girls to be couped up in the car with, this is a trip that I will never forget for sure! May 2004. Holland.

Arrange a photo strip

Where does the open road take you? Kim and her friends took time out for a girls' weekend to find out. Kim recorded the weekend with a twist on the typical photo collage. Printing her photos in black and white and arranging them to resemble old-time photo strips makes for a lively layout appropriate for the theme. Kim added color to the page with dynamic patterned paper and a large arrow-shaped journaling box that highlights the photos.

by Kim Moreno

Supplies: Cardstock (Core'dinations); patterned paper, roller stamps, stickers, bling (Glitz Designs); chipboard (EK Success); brads (American Crafts); journaling template (Designer Digitals); Misc: ink, decorative scissors

blueberries

flowers

musicians

THE TALLBOYS
IT TAKES A VILLAGE
TO TUNE A BANJO

38

veggies

Carrots
$2.50/bunch

Even though we live in Seattle it seems like we hardly ever get down to *Pikes Place*. At least once a year we try to remember to go down and see what's new there. Our *favorites* are the fresh veggies and huge bouquets of flowers. We also love to check out the art.

Pikes Place Market

Fresh

8/24/2008

Take a neighborhood vacation

Summer is full of special events like vacation and summer camp, but the everyday events can make for special layouts, too. The sun is shining and the days are long, so pack your camera and explore your own neighborhood. In Marie's layout, she admits that Pike Place Market is right in her backyard, but she hardly ever goes there. She proves that you don't need to hop on a plane to take a vacation! Often the best treasures—and potential for great pages—are hidden right under our noses.

by Marie Lottermoser

Supplies: Kit and stamp brushes by Rhonna Farrer (Two Peas in a Bucket); kit by Tia Bennett (Two Peas in a Bucket)

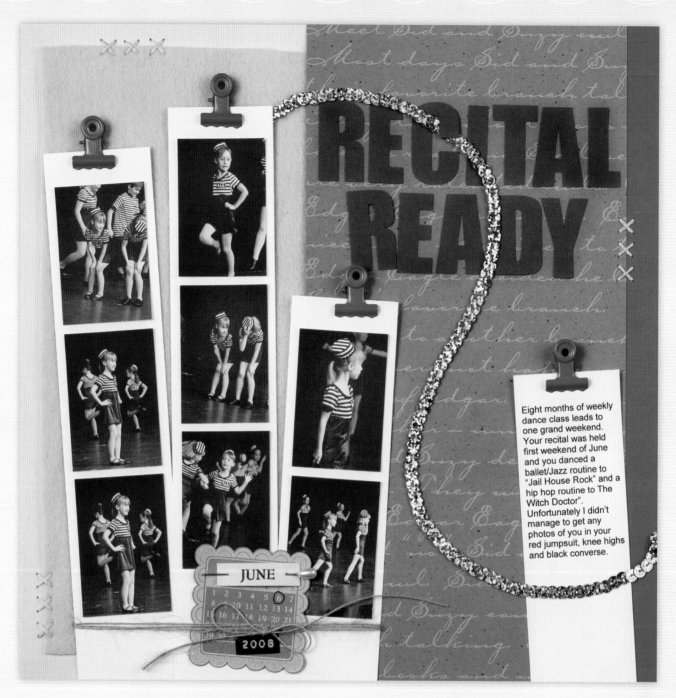

Eight months of weekly dance class leads to one grand weekend. Your recital was held first weekend of June and you danced a ballet/Jazz routine to "Jail House Rock" and a hip hop routine to The Witch Doctor". Unfortunately I didn't manage to get any photos of you in your red jumpsuit, knee highs and black converse.

JUNE
1 2 3 4 5 6 7
8 9 10 11 12 13 14
15 16 17 18 19 20 21
22 23 24 25 26 27 28
29 30
2008

Hit the fabric store

Summer loves to add texture to her layouts. So when she spotted these photos of her daughter's dance recital, she knew the extra texture of felt and sequins was going to be the perfect addition to help her layout shine. Hit the aisles of the fabric store to find stand-out embellishments for your layouts. On a layout like Summer's, you can also add leftover materials from a child's outfit or costume.

by Summer Fullerton

Supplies: Cardstock; patterned paper, twine, stamp (Jillibean Soup); felt, sequins (Jo-Ann); metal clips (Making Memories); floss (DMC); Misc: ink

Send along a camera

Growing up, Summer went to camp a handful of times, but the only memories she has are in her head. Laura was fortunate enough to get these awesome photos from her son's week at Boy Scout camp and record his experiences on this layout. Send your child to camp with a disposable camera so that even when you can't be there the memories can be documented on film—and in your album.

by Laura Ping

Supplies: letters (Purple Tulip Designs); binder clip, notebook paper by Gina Cabrera (Designer Digitals); tag by Katie Pertiet (Designer Digitals); Misc: clip art

Record spontaneity

It's scrapping the big summer events that can get repetitive, so look to spontaneous activities for fresh page ideas. Lisa's layout here caught our attention because of its different topic and multi-photo design. The cluster of smaller detail photos around a large group shot really shows off the event. Her choice of title colors, inspired by the s'mores theme, is mouth-watering, and pulls together this warm, lighthearted summer layout.

by Lisa Risser

Supplies: Cardstock; patterned paper (Cosmo Cricket); alphas (American Craft); rub-ons (K&Co.); buttons (Sassafras Lass); star (Tin-Tiques); Misc: ink

Clowning around at Knoebels is Fun!

GIGGLE №204094

Steph, Macy, Jack & Jen having a blast at Knoebel's!

FUN for all

June 13-15, 2008

Keep a title moving

Summertime often means trips to a carnival, complete with cotton candy and super-fun rides. To match the energetic feel of a carnival or amusement park, use a creative title block as Rachael did: She re-created the movement from her photos right on her layout. Rachael also applied a unique look to her photos, using a vintage Photoshop action to give them a timeless look that complemented the page's theme. You can give your photos a similar look by sanding and distressing the edges with ink. Top off a carnival layout with ticket stubs and star accents.

by Rachael Chamberlain

Supplies: Cardstock; patterned paper (Scenic Route); specialty paper (Wintech International); ticket (Tim Holtz); glitter glue (Ranger); shimmer spray (LuminArte); die-cut (Provo Craft); software (Craft Edge)

String a Triangle Banner

WHAT YOU'LL NEED

patterned paper, paper trimmer or craft knife and mat, straightedge, pencil, hole punch or Crop-A-Dile, embroidery floss

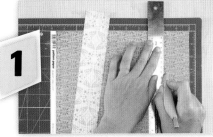

1

Cut three strips of 12" (30cm) patterned paper about 2" (5cm) wide. Use a different paper for each strip.

2

Mark every 2" (5cm) on the bottom and the top of the strip. The marks should be staggered: The top marks would be at 2", 4" (5cm, 10cm), etc., and the bottom marks at 1", 3" (3cm, 8cm), etc. Then connect the dots and cut out the triangles.

3

Punch holes in the upper two corners of the triangles. If you are using a Crop-A-Dile, you can easily punch through six triangles at once.

4

To connect the triangles, run a long strand of floss behind each (into the first hole and up through the second). Layer two sets of banners for an even more festive look.

Capture the essence

Summertime is packed with fun and family activities. Pony rides, carnival games and a carousel lured Michelle and her family to the county fair. You can capture the essence of the fair on your next layout by creating a flag banner from patterned paper as Michelle did. Bright bold colors and patterns are the perfect accompaniments for summer-time photos.

by Michelle Lanning

Supplies: Cardstock; patterned paper (Scenic Route, K&Co.); alphas (Cosmo Cricket, Making Memories); thread, stamps (Martha Stewart); rub-ons (Autumn Leaves); journaling block (Jennifer Peebles); Misc: ink

Alter an embellishment

We love the focus of Gina's creative Fourth of July layout. The focal photo highlighted by an altered metal frame pulls this piece together. In its original cream-colored state, the frame would have blended with the background. But Gina's dry-brush paint technique helps it—and the whole layout—stand out. When looking for the perfect accent for your next project, think about altering an item you otherwise might not have considered. Embellishments can easily be transformed by sanding, painting or inking.

by Gina Fensterer

Supplies: Cardstock (Core'dinations); patterned paper (Rusty Pickle); journaling paper, metal frame (Making Memories); tag (7Gypsies); sticker (Imagination Project); brads (Karen Foster); alphas (We R Memory Keepers)

Consider arrangement of photos

Ashley's Independence Day layout captures the emotion and spirit of the holiday. This layout boasts many traditional July Fourth elements— like plenty of stars and red, white and blue. But what really makes this layout sparkle is the juxtaposition of the photos. She coupled fireworks photos with the kids' reactions to the display. The arrangement makes the page come alive, like a real moment in time. Next time you add photos to a typical page, consider how they can work together to bring the layout to life.

by Ashley Harris

Supplies: Cardstock; patterned paper, chipboard (Scenic Route); buttons (Autumn Leaves); felt (Queen & Co.)

54

From Seth's convention blog:

The emotions continued on Thursday night. It was a great day at Invesco, and would have been an exciting enough event without Obama's speech. Besides, we'd already heard such incredible speeches from Bill and Hillary, and from Gore. I was frankly very proud to see the pool of talent in the Democratic Party. But Obama was just amazing that night, even if everyone predicted he would be anyway. My Blackberry, usually buzzing all day long with new e-mails, fell silent, and I realized that just about every human being I knew was watching the same thing I was watching. Being in the midst of 80,000 people, participating in something that felt like part speech, part U2 concert, part megachurch revival, was just astonishing. It felt like what politics is supposed to be. It had both substance and spectacle.

Great politicians have their own hooks. Reagan, as Peggy Noonan described him, could make you feel like he felt lucky to be with you. Bill Clinton can make you feel like he completely understands what you're going through. Obama makes you feel like you're part of a movement. I fully recognize that it's not a movement -- it's a candidacy. But it's a rare politician that can convey that feeling. Sometimes we support politicians for purely instrumental reasons -- we want lower taxes or particular favors or policies from government and figure we can get it from a particular politician. Sometimes we support politicians simply because they suck somewhat less than the people they're running against. But people actually enjoy the act of supporting Obama. You feel like you're part of something important and historical. That is rare.

the DNC 2008

Summer Scrapping Checklist

- ☐ Last day of school
- ☐ Graduation
- ☐ Father's Day
- ☐ Fourth of July
- ☐ Berry picking
- ☐ Bike riding
- ☐ Camping
- ☐ Family reunion
- ☐ Local festivals and fairs
- ☐ Outdoor activities like fishing and hiking
- ☐ Picnics and cookouts
- ☐ Summer sports such as golf, swimming or tennis
- ☐ Summer treats like ice cream, snow cones and frozen pops
- ☐ Vacations and road trips
- ☐ Water activities

Use a blog

Have you ever been a part of history? Vivian's husband was given a great opportunity to attend the Democratic National Convention and she created this layout recording his journey. She combined photos taken from a cell phone along with her husband's words from his blog. Blogs are a sign of the times—and also make journaling easy!—so try creating a timely layout using words from your own blog.

by Vivian Masket

Supplies: Cardstock; patterned paper (Scenic Route); alphas (American Crafts); fabric tab (Scrapworks); Misc: star punches, campaign button

DODGE PICKUP

(aka picking strawberries while dodging raindrops)

Simply say it

Summer means berries are in season and it's time to pack your camera and head for the fields. Take a simple approach like Terri did by getting creative with your title and embellishment. This layout says it all without overdoing it. The raindrop accents cut from patterned paper combined with great photos and a clever one-liner make this a fabulous layout that can be easily created in one hour or less.

by Terri Davenport

Supplies: Cardstock; patterned paper, chipboard (American Crafts); Misc: punch

Use kraft cardstock

May sent us this darling layout featuring her daughter and a garden full of fresh tomatoes. A kraft cardstock background is a simple but fresh addition to any page. The neutral color allows photos to shine, and its raw look is especially appropriate for garden-themed layouts. May combined the kraft paper with simple red accents that make the photos pop. The small clusters of buttons with a flourish stamped image are reminiscent of tomatoes on the vine.

by May Flaum

Supplies: Cardstock; alphas (Heidi Grace); chipboard (American Crafts); brad (Making Memories); buttons (Making Memories, Autumn Leaves); Misc: punch, ribbon, thread, tag, lined paper

Get inspired by magazines

Tricia's bountiful garden is a colorful example of what many of us wish to grow. On this layout she highlights the colorful bounty against a black background. Tricia was inspired by an advertisement in a magazine and used it as the foundation for the page. So, when searching for creative inspiration, look no further than your stash of magazines or catalogs for an endless number of ideas.

by Tricia Gorden

Supplies: Cardstock; patterned paper (Miss Elizabeth's); die-cut (Provo Craft); Misc: acrylic paint

2008 was the first year that we actually went to the Pickle fest in St. Joe, IN. We had been to the factory, but never the festival. We tried pickle ice cream, pickle popcorn + had a really fun day. No wonder though... We love pickles!!

Pickle ice cream →

strong

Pickle People Contest

august

upside down storage!!

LIFE IS GOOD

(lots of) cucumbers →

the final product

more pickle ice cream!!

BRAVE

Pickle Fest

Scrap a different two-page layout

When scrapbooking multiple photos we often visualize the background as one large 12" × 24" (30cm × 61cm) canvas. Shannon's fun-filled page reminds us that great two-page layouts don't have to be split over the seam. Shannon used two large photo blocks and connected the pages visually by using the same papers and elements on each side of the layout. It goes to show that fresh ideas don't take much—just a little something different.

by Shannon Blinn

Supplies: Cardstock; patterned paper (Making Memories, Scenic Route); lace cardstock (KI Memories); chipboard (Scenic Route); letters (American Crafts)

Nature's Beauty
a celebration

Isn't this lovely? What a GREAT way to celebrate summer! There haven't been a lot of warm, sunny days this year, but this particular Saturday was just PERFECT. Marlene took me to Mud Lake in Ottawa's west end, and she taught me how to use the manual setting on my digital SLR. I got to try out her collection of lenses (telephoto, macro, wide angle), and I pushed my creativity way beyond my comfort zone by photographing insects, birds, flowers and other non-people subjects. I enjoyed our walk through the nature preserve, and Marlene and I had a chance to catch up on one another's busy lives. I can't imagine a more perfect summer morning... all without travelling beyond city limits. I ♡ summer in Ottawa. Aug 16, 2008

House titles in photos

Enlarged scenic photos make a great backdrop for titles or journaling. Barb found the perfect home for her title in the empty space of a summer photo. She created the hybrid title by adding text digitally to the photo before printing it, and completing the title with tiny letter stickers. You can add text to photos using an image-editing or word processing program, but if you aren't computer savvy, you can achieve a similar look using rub-ons or stickers.

by Barb Wong

Supplies: Cardstock; patterned paper (Scrapworks); alphas (EK Success); brads (BasicGrey); Misc: ink, punches

Mix it up

The beauty of summer weather isn't just the warmth but the moments that are captured under the sun. These precious memories that Milagros preserved certainly illustrate the beauty of summer. The wonderful close-up photo of the butterfly really caught our eye, and Milagros captured the theme well with her mix of different types of embellishments—beaded, paper, flocked, epoxy, glittered and more. On your next summer page, add texture and create interest by mixing types of embellishments on the layout.

by Milagros C. Rivera

Supplies: Cardstock (Core'dinations); patterned paper (Heidi Swapp); journaling sheet, metal sign, ribbon (Making Memories); epoxy sticker, butterfly clip (KI Memories); flowers (Prima); brads (Doodlebug); butterflies (Maya Road); Misc: beads, wire

JOURNALING TRANSLATION

The marvel behind the chrysalis. This beautiful Monarch butterfly was born at home and Mercedes freed it with her friend Clara.

The scrapbook layout reads: **BUILD • LAUNCH • FLY**

Photo caption on layout: Flying kites and the Oregon coast go hand in hand. The wide expansive beaches and the wild winds make for perfect kite flying conditions. Today was an A+ day for kite flying. The plus being awarded for the sun that is so infrequent at the coast. Grant and Corinne had a blast flying their fancy new kites up and down the beach. Fort Stevens July 2007

Craft a summertime accent

Make your next summer layout pop with a creative handmade embellishment that brings the activity to life. All you have to do is dig into your stash of paper scraps and get creative. Summer made this summer-inspired layout featuring photos of her family flying kites at the Oregon coast. To complement the photos, she crafted a tiny kite from scraps of paper, buttons and ribbon. In addition, her title is a creative take on captions for the photos. Try making your own summertime accents, like a butterfly, sailboat or shining sun.

by Summer Fullerton

Supplies: Cardstock; patterned paper (Jillibean Soup, October Afternoon, Pink Paislee); buttons (SEI); brads (Creative Café); stamp, twine (Jillibean Soup); measuring tape accent, ribbon (Making Memories); alpha (QuicKutz); floss (DMC); Misc: ink, punch, corner rounder

Show a sequence

We often spend so much time scrapbooking our children that we forget to record the things that make us who we are. Brenda's layout pops as the perfect example of how to scrap a summertime passion. The lively page shows a sequence of action that makes it come alive. Brenda used image-editing software to add captions to her photos before printing them; these words tell the story in a creative, active way. Brenda also embellished the page with perfectly themed accents, including a leaf stamp she fashioned from an actual leaf.

by Brenda Hurd

Supplies: Cardstock; patterned paper (Scenic Route, Prima Marketing); alphas (Making Memories); border (Bazzill); felt fish, chipboard (Fancy Pants); gems (Kaisercraft); thread (DMC); sequins (Scarlet Lime); Misc: acrylic paint

Craft a Stamp from Nature

WHAT YOU'LL NEED

acrylic stamping block, dry adhesive, plant piece, acrylic paint, foam brush, foam mat

1 Add dry adhesive to an acrylic block. Place the piece of plant on the adhesive to hold it in place.

2 Cover the plant generously with acrylic paint using a foam brush.

3 Place a foam mat under your project. Then stamp the plant image.

Add unexpected embellishments

Birthday layouts can be taken in many different directions. Kim's page is the perfect example of a unique birthday layout. By creating a link between her photos, journaling and accents, this layout stands out from the pack. Her lighthearted, warm journaling mentions the islands, and Kim took this idea one step further by topping off the layout with fun island touches such as palm tree die-cuts and fun stitching. Make your next birthday layout stand out by reaching for non-traditional accents to enhance your story.

by Kim Watson

Supplies: Cardstock; patterned papers (Chatterbox, Tinkering Ink, Scenic Route); stickers (Heidi Swapp); alphas (Tinkering Ink, American Crafts); buttons (Autumn Leaves); shrink-plastic star (Around the Block); spotted ribbon, metal embellishment (Making Memories); stamp (Croxley); Misc: ink, corner rounder, decorative scissors

Highlight the words

Going to the chapel this summer? Along with the typical flowers and black-and-white wedding photos, add a twist to your background. On her bright and happy wedding layout, Marci added a dictionary-page backdrop she made by copying dictionary pages directly onto cardstock. Then she cleverly used watercolors to highlight the words *wedding* and *day* that are featured in the background paper. Marci also employed her embroidery skills—adding French knots to the center of each flower—to provide a new take on dressing up flowers.

by Marci Lambert

Supplies: Cardstock; alphas (Making Memories); chipboard letters (American Crafts); border stickers (Hambly Screen Prints); flowers (Prima Marketing); watercolors (Loew-Cornell)

Pile on the texture

So much care goes into all those wedding details that the day deserves a page highlighting them. Weddings are extra-special, so take care to produce an extra-special wedding page like Francine's, which boasts fresh colors, lots of texture and rich details. Layers of ribbon, paper lace, velvet letters, textured paper and fancy stitching all add to the richness of the layout.

by Francine Clouden

Supplies: Cardstock; patterned paper (Prima); alphas (American Crafts); spray ink (Tattered Angels, Stewart Superior); gem (Heidi Swapp); chipboard (Fancy Pants); journaling spot (Luxe Designs); ribbon (Imaginisce); paper lace (K&Co.); flower (Maya Road)

Record your anniversary

Renee's layout shows off photos from a Caribbean vacation celebrating more than 10 years of marriage. Even if you don't celebrate with an elaborate vacation you can still scrapbook the event. If it's just dinner and a movie or your one-month anniversary, simply snap a few photos and you have the start of a great seasonal layout. Create an anniversary page like Renee to celebrate your years, using products that reflect the mood of your photos.

by Renee Morris-Dezember

Supplies: Cardstock; patterned paper, die-cuts (October Afternoon); ribbon, alphas (Making Memories); felt, button (Chatterbox); Misc: ink

Communicate with large-scale accents

Reaching 10 years of marriage is a big event, one that calls for big ideas. Use large-scale accents, as Summer did, to communicate the importance of a special day. Summer did this by cutting out a large flower from a bold patterned paper. Pairing the large-scale accent with black-and-white photos and simple kraft paper makes for a balanced composition.

By Summer Ford

Supplies: Cardstock; patterned paper (Tinkering Ink); rub-ons (Tinkering Ink, Autumn Leaves); chipboard (All My Memories); stamps (Hero Arts); brads, photo turns (Making Memories); buttons (Darice); Misc: ink

Living in Florida, we've become used to the preparations that need to be taken every time a hurricane starts making its way to our state. We always do our best to make sure our family has everything in order just in case one was hit us directly. Luckily, we haven't had one come close enough to need to use many supplies, but we feel good knowing that we are always prepared. These precautions seem to have become a late summer ritual these past few years. We like the peace of mind knowing that we are ready for the worst, but are so glad that we haven't had to experience it.

in the event of a HURRiCaNe

Scrap summer rituals

Scrapbooks can be used to memorialize the good, the bad and the ugly. Linda sent us this look into how her family prepares for a hurricane. This layout is a great reminder to scrapbook those seasonal summer rituals. Linda used a well-balanced combination of map-themed product and dark colors, giving her layout a stormy feel. Get creative with your title as Linda did by layering mesh over chipboard letters.

by Linda Harrison

Supplies: Cardstock; patterned paper (Tinkering Ink); brads (Making Memories); alphas (Doodlebug, BasicGrey); mesh (Magic Mesh); paper clip (KI Memories); rub-ons (Art Warehouse)

Use a grid design

Laina's pool party layout packs a punch with 12 photos and a large pirate ship. The page's grid design is an effective way to maximize space on a layout. To keep multiple colorful photos from becoming overwhelming, place simple patterned paper in a few of the grid spaces. Also, juxtapose a collage of smaller photos and accents with one oversized element like this pirate ship. Aaargh!

by Laina Lamb

Supplies: Cardstock; patterned papers (Die Cuts With A View, KI Memories); overlay (Hambly); ribbon (KI Memories); rub-ons (BasicGrey, American Crafts); stickers (American Crafts, Fiskars); chipboard (Heidi Swapp); Misc: gem heart, staples

Jot it Down

Get a jumpstart on your scrapbooking projects by carrying a journal with you all summer long. Use the journaling while on vacation to record trip details you might otherwise have forgotten when you get around to scrapbooking those stacks of vacation photos. Keep a journal in your purse or car to record the simple things from those lazy summer days like silly quotes and special moments. A journal is a wonderful resource tool no matter what time of year it is.

Assemble a border of tags

What would summer be without time spent at the beach? We were completely taken in by Sherry's stunning photos of her children enjoying the ocean. The orange, teal and green color scheme on her layout is the perfect complement for her photos. On your next beach-themed layout, assemble a border from transparencies and metal tag rims. Mix up patterns and shapes to make a fresh and fun embellishment for the page—perfect for the ocean.

by Sherry Steveson

Supplies: Cardstock; patterned paper (Fancy Pants, Autumn Leaves, Daisy D's); alphas, chipboard letters (American Crafts); tags (Making Memories); transparency (Hambly)

Make a Metal-Rimmed Tag

WHAT YOU'LL NEED

transparency, pen (like American Crafts' Slick Writer), scissors, metal tag, Tag Maker and template (by Making Memories)

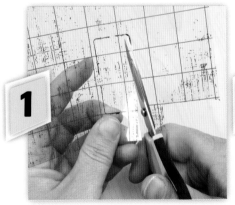

1 Trace around the Tag Maker template using a pen that won't smear (such as American Crafts' Slick Writer). Cut out the shape just inside the lines; this allows the transparency to fit better inside the tag.

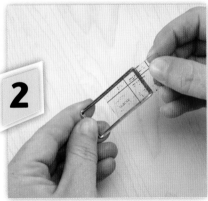

2 Slide the transparency shape into the metal tag frame. You may need to trim the edges down just a bit more to allow for a perfect fit.

3 Place one end of the metal tag into the Tag Maker and gently squeeze the tool to flatten and close the edges. Repeat with the other end.

Variation: If you don't have a Tag Maker, use an ordinary metal-rimmed tag. Simply cut out the white center and then glue a piece of transparency to the back side of the metal rim.

i just LOVE

autumn

MEMO
Autumn is by far my
favourite of all the
seasons. The bright
blue skies, the clean,
crisp air & the beautiful
leaves in those
gorgeous, happy colours.

Chapter 3

Fall

The blistering summer days fade into crisp mornings with dew-kissed grass. It's fall, with its spectacular array of falling leaves, hot apple cider and pumpkin pie. Get inspired by the palette of the season and reach for warm hues and rich textures. To keep fall layouts fresh, add cozy details as in Christine Rumley's blanket stitching on page 76. Or keep it simple as Stacey Michaud did on page 86. In this chapter, join us on a tour through fall from the first day of school through Thanksgiving and everything in between.

NINTH GRADE

SIXTH GRADE

FOURTH GRADE

Before the lunches are packed &
the school bell rings welcoming
a new school year,
the boys know the back-to-school
drill. They meet me in the backyard
for the annual

FIRST DAY photos

REACH FOR THE STARS

Create repetition

Fall layouts tend to look the same from year to year, but in the case of first-day photos, that's the whole point! The cleverness of a back-to-school page is the repetition, whether it's like Tracy's layouts showing her three sons in the same spot or whether the page shows one child from a succession of years. Whatever method inspires you, be sure to note the location and the ritual as Tracy did.

by Tracy Schmitt

Supplies: Cardstock; patterned paper (KI Memories); alphas (American Crafts); chipboard (KI Memories, Junkitz); labels (Dymo); Misc: ink, acrylic paint, notebook paper, staples, button

Every year for the last 6 years we have gone through the "back to school" routine of buying supplies, new shoes, new back packs, etc. And every year, as hard as it is to let you go, I've always had someone home to keep me company. Not this year...

I'm letting you all go, and it makes me sad. August 2008

every year

Record your emotions

Since back to school comes around every year, if you have kids, you probably scrap the subject every year. Of course, there are the requisite back to school photos to scrap—so go ahead and record them. But also use the creative process as a time to reflect: How do you feel about the kids leaving? What memories of your own childhood does it trigger? What are you looking forward to this school year? We love Aly's fresh approach to back to school—with journaling that describes her feelings about sending her youngest off to school for the first time. It's touching and really inspires.

by Aly Dosdall

Supplies: Cardstock; journaling strips (Dunia); chipboard letter by Celeste Rockwood-Jones and Natalie Malan (PC Layers); mini kit by Krystal Hartley (www.krystalhartley.blogspot.com)

Make a list

We love Kim's fresh approach to documenting her daughter heading off to fifth grade. She could have gone the traditional route with a focus on starting school. Instead, she centered this layout around the must-haves for the first day. Try Kim's checklist technique on your own back-to-school layout. Or expand upon the theme with a layout about back-to-school shopping. Note Kim's use of simple school-themed product—such as a pencil stamp, apple and grid papers, and a notebook border punch—that enhance the layout's theme.

by Kim Moreno

Supplies: Cardstock (Core'dinations); patterned paper (October Afternoon); chipboard (Making Memories); stickers (Making Memories, October Afternoon); gems (Kaisercraft); stamp, ribbon (Maya Road); tag (Creative Imaginations); Misc: ink, punch, thread

Fall Scrapping Checklist

- [ ] Back to school
- [ ] Labor Day
- [ ] Harvest parties
- [ ] Carving pumpkins
- [ ] Halloween activities
- [ ] Veteran's Day
- [ ] Thanksgiving
- [ ] Apple picking
- [ ] Enjoying fall treats like apple cider, pumpkin pie and caramel apples
- [ ] Fall leaves
- [ ] Fall sports such as football, soccer, cross country and cheerleading
- [ ] Hayrides
- [ ] Homecoming
- [ ] Homecoming festivities
- [ ] Planting bulbs
- [ ] Visit to the pumpkin patch

Get past the first day

After the first day of school has passed and the routines settle in, we tend to put down our cameras. But there is still an entire school year to remember! While her daughter was doing homework one afternoon, Summer snapped several shots to document the process. The end result is this two-page layout featuring primary colors, apple accents and lined paper. Don't let your school layouts end in September. Document homework time as Summer did, or record your child's favorite subject, after-school activities or school friendships.

by Summer Fullerton

Supplies: Cardstock; patterned paper, apple (October Afternoon); floss (DMC); alphas, brads (BasicGrey); sticker (7Gypsies); buttons (Making Memories); Misc: scallop punch, staples

Go for the obvious

How could we resist Julie's layout documenting an annual rubber duckie derby? This layout is a wonderful reminder of those yearly but quirky moments that provide the unexpected pages for our scrapbooks. The yellow paper, bubbly accents and duck-shaped journaling bring this layout to life. Sometimes, we get wrapped up in the idea that our layouts should be complex. This layout reminds us that the obvious embellishment, like a rubber duck, is sometimes the best.

by Julie White

Supplies: Splish Splash Kit by Rhonna Farrer (Two Peas in a Bucket); stitches by Shalae Tippetts (ScrapSimple Tools); papers, duck shape for text, title letter by Julie White; Misc: Gill Sans and Zapfino fonts

Create a patchwork title

by Shannon Taylor

Shannon sent us this two-page layout that showcases a fall family tradition. When scrapping fall photos, create lots of layers to evoke warmth. For your own cozy layout, try Shannon's technique for building a title with depth. On cardstock, draw a box to fit your title. Cut strips of different patterned papers and adhere them to the box, creating the look of a patchwork quilt. Cut out the box, trimming the strips as needed.

Supplies: Patterned paper (A2Z Essentials, American Crafts, BasicGrey, Junkitz, KI Memories, My Mind's Eye, Sandylion); digital paper by Shannon Freeman (Two Peas in a Bucket); alphas (American Crafts); die-cut (Pink Paislee); rub-ons (Maya Road); stamp (Junkitz); chipboard (Sandy Lion)

Grandma Frieda's

honeycake

family
traditions
baking

now and then

Every year we make a honeycake on Rosh Hashanah, ringing in the Jewish New Year with sweetness. We always use my Grandma Frieda's recipe – lots of honey, strong coffee, nuts, and raisins. Not long after Rosh Hashanah last year Grandma Frieda passed away. I am sure that our honeycake tradition will acquire a new layer of meaning this year as we connect not only with our heritage, but with Grandma Frieda, and all of the fond memories we have of time spent with her.

Sept 2007

Draw a border

Every year, Vivian celebrates Rosh Hashanah by baking a family recipe for honeycake, an event she recorded on this sweet and simple layout. Even when you don't have many photos to scrap, you can still create a memorable layout for your album by using simple designs and heartfelt journaling. Vivian grounded her layout by adding a hand-drawn border in pen. This can be replicated on any layout and at any skill level. For more advanced scrapbookers, try hand sewing or machine stitching a border.

by Vivian Masket

Supplies: Cardstock; patterned paper (Scenic Route, October Afternoon); stickers (American Crafts, October Afternoon); chipboard (KI Memories); red tab, epoxy sticker (Creative Imaginations); Misc: punch

Stitch the edges

Autumn in Australia actually begins in March, while the buds are beginning to bloom in the United States. Whatever the month, there is something magical when the air turns clean and crisp and the leaves begin to turn. Fall is a favorite season of many of us, including Christine, and she shares this on her layout. Create a cozy feeling on your own fall layout by using creative stitching. Christine's use of a blanket stitch as a border reminds us of a big fluffy blanket or sweater—just in time for autumn.

by Christine Rumley

Supplies: Patterned paper (Stampin' UP!, Scenic Route, My Mind's Eye); alphas (SEI, Making Memories); journaling blocks (October Afternoon, Jenni Bowlin Studios); floss (DMC)

Learn the Blanket Stitch

1 Place a foam mat under the layout. Using a thumbtack or paper piercer, punch small holes along the edge of the page. The holes should be about ¼" (6mm) from the edge of the page. You can space them as desired; these are about ½" (1cm) apart.

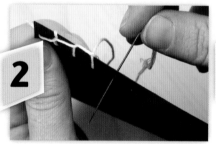

2 Thread the needle and knot the end of the floss. Insert the needle through the hole from behind and then insert it into the next hole from the front. Do not pull the floss tight.

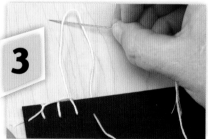

3 Slide the needle through the loop in the floss.

Pull the floss taut. Repeat steps 2–4 to continue the stitch. **4**

are we blowing the leaves?

Scrap fall chores

Take Nicole's approach to your next seasonal layout and scrapbook a family chore, like bagging up those leaves. Build your layout using a wonderfully rich fall color scheme topped off with leaf accents. Add premade, lifelike leaves like Nicole did, or get out your paper punches or die-cut machine to make your own. Be sure to gather several leaves for a true-to-life take on the season.

by Nicole Martel

Supplies: Cardstock; patterned paper (October Afternoon); flowers (Prima Marketing, Creative Imaginations); alphas (American Crafts); button (Creative Imaginations)

Reach for the stars

Basketball doesn't really scream "fall," but in the autumn, Kim sat in the bleachers watching her son play basketball and snapping photos. While creating this page, Kim realized she was short on basketball-themed product, so she reached for the stars instead. Basic products such as star patterned paper, shapes and accents are perfect for sports layouts. And it goes to show that special layouts don't always require special product.

by Kim Moreno

Supplies: Cardstock (Core'dinations); patterned paper (Dream Street Papers); acrylic (Pageframe Designs); eyelets (American Crafts); stick pins (Fancy Pants Designs); brads (Bazzill); stickers (Sonburn); Misc: punch, decorative scissors, thread

Attach a Transparent Shape

WHAT YOU'LL NEED

acrylic shape, eyelet, Crop-A-Dile

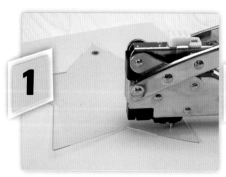

1

Set the acrylic shape on the background. Then punch a hole through the acrylic and background simultaneously, using the Crop-A-Dile.

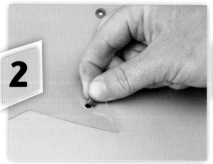

2

Place the eyelet through the acrylic shape and background.

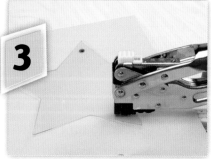

3

Use the Crop-A-Dile to crimp the eyelet closed. Remember to insert the Crop-A-Dile's "pointy" end into the eyelet's hole on top.

Skip the themed product

Veronica sent us this layout documenting a professional football game she and her son attended. Like Kim's basketball layout on the previous page, this layout conveys the sports theme without using themed product. Allow yourself to take this approach on your next layout, and reach for your favorite papers, even when they might not seem to "match" your photos. You're guaranteed to create an interesting page that breaks the rules.

by Veronica Jennings

Supplies: Cardstock; patterned paper (Cosmo Cricket, Creative Imaginations, Making Memories); tags (Elle's Studio); rub-ons (Fontwerks, Jenni Bowlin Studios); felt (Jenni Bowlin Studios); Misc: acrylic paint

Record the nitty gritty

Fall brings the start of football season. Kim Frantz's husband doesn't just watch football, he spends his weekend getting dirty making the calls that make the game happen. We loved the down and dirty spirit of this layout captured by a pair of photos. When you hit the field to take photos of your next sporting event, capture the easy-to-forget details, like dirty cleats, muddy jerseys, sideline antics and water breaks.

by Kim Frantz

Supplies: Cardstock; patterned paper (BasicGrey, Cosmo Cricket, KI Memories); buttons (Dress It Up); chipboard (Making Memories, Scenic Route, WorldWin); dies (Provo Craft); rub-ons (American Crafts); stickers (SEI); Misc: cardboard, chalk, floss

Balance out the orange

No fall scrapbook album is complete without pumpkin photos. To make sure pages don't drown in a sea of orange, use neutral patterned papers and a background trimmed in color. Then add pops of additional color that complement the photos, like the aqua flowers Paula used on this adorable page. To make the page even more special, Paula hand-cut the flowers from a pretty patterned paper.

by Paula Gilarde

Supplies: Cardstock; alphas (Heidi Swapp); patterned papers (October Afternoon, 7Gypsies, Autumn Leaves); chipboard (Li'l Davis Designs); ribbon (Autumn Leaves)

Pick a pair of pictures

Visiting the pumpkin patch is a favorite fall activity that can leave a scrapper with a memory card full of photos. Amy's simple layout shows that there's no need to be overwhelmed by lots of pictures. Pairing one great scenic photo with a photo of her child is all Amy needed to perfectly capture the memory and make a beautiful page. Sometimes, less is more and will make your pages feel clean and uncluttered.

by Amy Martin

Supplies: Papers, overlay, elements (Little Dreamer Designs); ribbon, label by Jackie Eckles (Little Dreamer Designs)

Inside the layout image: **fall view** — I love everything about fall. The beautiful harvest colors. The ripe apples hanging on the trees. The bright orange pumpkins. The leaves changing colors. Warm days. Crisp nights.

Use time-saving tricks

Stick to Heather's simple formula and scrap those fall photos in a flash! Her layout is packed with all kinds of time-saving tricks like using photos straight from the processor, limiting herself to the barest of supplies, journaling by hand and leaving chipboard in its raw state. After all, when the beauty of photos speak for themselves why complicate things? You already have a pile of fall leaves to tackle; make it simple to scrap that pile of fall photos.

by Heather Bowser

Supplies: Cardstock; patterned paper (KI Memories); ribbon, alphas (American Crafts); chipboard (Maya Road)

Go Back to School

If you just started scrapbooking—or even you've been at it for years—take a back-to-school cue from your kids and hit the scrapbook classroom. This fall, while your kids are in class, check out your local scrapbook store for classes. If you'd rather learn from the comfort of your scrap room, go online to find web-based workshops. Many online retailers and scrapbooking blogs have classes and tutorials. Sites such as www.twopeasinabucket.com, www.bigpicture scrapbooking.com, www.debbiehodge.com and even YouTube offer classes and tutorials on just about every topic, from photography to stamping to organizing.

Choose not-so-typical colors

October 31 is the grand finale of a whole month full of activities that are just begging to be scrapbooked. Summer snapped these photos of her son carving a pumpkin to adorn the family's front porch. What makes this layout stand out is Summer's use of not-so-typical Halloween colors—blue and green really makes the orange photos pop. For a different take on scrapbooking Halloween, dig out that stash of plain ol' paper. If you still want to use themed paper, make room for generic patterns by cutting out parts of the Halloween paper and layering it over the other. It'll be a real treat!

by Summer Fullerton

Supplies: Cardstock; patterned paper (BasicGrey, Scenic Route, Making Memories); alphas (Crate Paper, Making Memories, Doodlebug Designs); rhinestones (Kaizer Craft); stickers (Daisy D's)

Make Paper Cut-Outs That Pop

WHAT YOU'LL NEED

two patterned papers (one with a pattern to cut [flocking optional] and one in a contrasting color), craft knife, craft mat

1

Set the paper on the mat. Using a craft knife, carefully cut away the paper in between the pattern. (Using flocked paper will make cutting easier as the ridges will help guide the knife.)

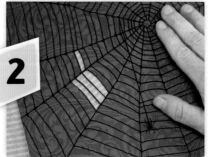

2

Layer the cut-out paper on top of a contrasting piece of paper.

Variation
For a similar look without the hassle, place a piece of die-cut paper over the contrasting piece of paper.

Stage a sunlit shoot

Do you get stuck with blurry, poorly lit photos of your kids on Halloween? Eliminate the issue and make a better Halloween page using Kimber's bright idea: Have kids dress early for the big night and stage a photo shoot out in the light of day. This allowed Kimber's kids to not only get into character for the big night but also for her to capture all the fun before the sun went down.

by Kimber McGray

Supplies: Cardstock; patterned paper, metal, ribbon, chipboard, flocking (We R Memory Keepers); Misc: ink

I love Guy Fawkes Day! It's one of the first weekends in the year that the BBQ comes back out from hiding after a long winter. It's a social time with no pressure of buying gifts or dressing up. The kids love it and I get to hang out with the neighbours. We usually have a street gathering on the weekend closest to the 5th of November, which is the real Guy Fawkes Day. We have a few drinks and a BBQ. When it gets dark we let the kids play with the sparklers and we let off fireworks for them to watch. Although I know Guy Fawkes Day is a British tradition dating back hundreds of years, I am yet to tell the kids of its significance. For now we'll just enjoy the social side of it!

guy fawkes nz
Trina and Andy.
7th November 2004

Get inspired

Guy Fawkes Day is a tradition celebrated with bonfires and fireworks in New Zealand. Guy Fawkes Day may be unfamiliar to Americans, but Nic's layouts depicting the holiday could easily be mistaken for a more familiar July 4th page. Nic uses the layout to tell about her family's traditions for Guy Fawkes Day. She also uses lots of sparkle on the page to highlight the lights in the photos. Even if you don't live in New Zealand, you can translate Nic's techniques onto any holiday layout to make a spectacular page.

by Nic Howard

Supplies: Cardstock; patterned paper (BasicGrey, Pink Paislee); chipboard letters (BasicGrey, Making Memories); chipboard (Heidi Swapp); jewels (Queen & Co.); ticket (Jenni Bowlin); dimensional medium (Plaid); rub-ons (Adornit)

obviously being
only thirteen
Hayden cannot
vote in the
upcoming election,
but he definitely
has strong
political opinions.
He is quite
sure he knows
what is best
for our country
and who would
be best to lead.
as adults we
respect his
opinions and
make our decision
to be heard by
casting our ballot
on election day.
be heard.
declare yourself.
vote.

DECLARE YOURSELF

7/2008

Break the rules

When you think of November, you probably think of pumpkins and turkey. But let's not forget it's also the time when we take to the polls to vote. Voting day may not seem that special, but years from now you'll be glad you recorded a moment in history. Mary sent us this eye-catching layout about her teenaged son's political views. What makes the layout striking is its simplicity—the single large photo, bold title and journaling. The "rules" tell us to get a lot of photos on a page, but sometimes one photo is all you need, especially when you don't have a lot of photos in the first place.

by Mary Rogers

Supplies: Paper by Katie Pertiet (Designer Digitals); painted edges, journaling lines by Anna Aspnes (Designer Digitals); 28 days later font (dafont.com); Pea Marcie's Skinny Print font (Kevin and Amanda)

Use a cardstock background

The holiday of choice at Stacey's house is Thanksgiving. The family's day begins early in the morning with fellowship and lots of turkey—details that she records on this page. Stacey included a variety of snapshots from the entire day, which is pretty typical of a holiday layout. To make sure photos don't get lost on a busy page, use a basic cardstock background highlighted with strips of patterned paper. Add a few small embellishments and simple journaling, and you're good to go!

by Stacey Michaud

Supplies: Cardstock; patterned paper (GCD); buttons (Autumn Leaves); alphas (American Crafts); felt (KI Memories); journaling card (My Mind's Eye); rub-ons (Deja Views); stickers, tickets (Making Memories); clip (Staples)

Pick a new tradition

This year, when faced with scrapbooking yet another round of Thanksgiving photos, try a new approach. Michele's layout details how her family spends their Thanksgiving every year. Have you ever sat down to write about your traditions? Every family celebrates the holidays in their own way, so record special rituals, share recipes or tell old family stories. Pick a different one to tell every year so that Thanksgiving layouts never become dull.

by Michele Skinner

Supplies: Cardstock; patterned paper (My Mind's Eye, October Afternoon); alphas (Doodlebug, American Crafts); thread (DMC)

Record your senses

Take your next holiday layout to a new level by scrapbooking photos that evoke the emotion of the holiday. Whether it's the aroma of pumpkin pie or the snowflakes falling at Christmas, each holiday can take us on a journey of the senses. Michelle takes us on such a journey, recording the details of a country Thanksgiving. Take time to explore the sights and sounds of your own holidays though photos. Your end result will be a glorious layout you will enjoy for a lifetime.

by Michelle Engel

Supplies: Cardstock; patterned paper (BoBunny Press); alphas (American Crafts); brads (Imaginisce); ribbon (Beau Regards); Misc: photo hanger

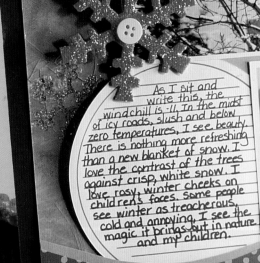

As I sit and write this, the windchill is -11. In the midst of icy roads, slush and below zero temperatures, I see beauty. There is nothing more refreshing than a new blanket of snow. I love the contrast of the trees against crisp, white snow. I love rosy, winter cheeks on children's faces. Some people see winter as treacherous, cold and annoying. I see the magic it brings out in nature and my children.

winter magic

Chapter 4

Winter

Last winter, Summer was snowed in for almost a week. It was the perfect opportunity to do a little scrapbooking—some holiday music was all she needed to get to work. We all tend to scrapbook more during the winter months. The shorter days and blustery weather provide the perfect excuse to hole up in your scrap space. So why not start this chapter outlining some of the ways you can scrapbook the many things you do this time of year? To start, check out Sabrina Ropp's creative cropping on page 95 and Lisa Dorsey's spectacular background treatment on page 104. Stepping outside your comfort zone is a surefire way to get fresh winter pages and scrap the holidays, snow fun, winter sports and more.

chocolate filled

twenty·four days

Simple .99 cent advent calendars are the most popular purchases I make every year. Each night you punch open a little window to reveal a tiny morsel of chocolate. You and Grant compare the embossed designs on your candy and make predictions of what the next night might bring. Tonight was the 4th of many chocolate filled days before Christmas.

Corinne 12/04/07

Scrap the little things

Make holiday albums exciting this year by snapping photos of all the little things you do to celebrate. One evening, Summer picked up her camera while her daughter was opening the Advent calendar, though she wouldn't have normally thought to capture a moment like that. Whip out your own camera during mini-events like wrapping presents, unpacking ornaments or caroling around the block. Add extra zing when scrapping by choosing unexpected supplies—pink camouflage anyone?

by Summer Fullerton

Supplies: Cardstock; patterned paper (Tinkering Ink); eyelets (American Crafts); felt, stick pins (Fancy Pants); ribbon (May Arts); stickers (American Crafts, K&Co.); Misc: punches

{ YUm YUm }

Christmas Cookie Day has been a tradition in my family since before I was born. Every year on the day after Thanksgiving we bake Grandma Robison's yummy cookies, frost them with her out-of-this-world fondant icing, then let the kids (old and young alike) decorate them. The cookies rarely make it to see the light of the next day - we usually eat them as fast as we decorate them! Jack, Makele, Aunt Taryn, Dustin and Dakoda are pictured. November 23, 2007.

ChrisTmas Cookies

Make it sparkle

Scrapbooking your holiday traditions shouldn't be a chore. The holidays provide the perfect excuse to add some sparkle and pizzazz, so take inspiration for your next layout from Brenda. This layout is packed full of ideas you can use on your next holiday layout, no matter what the subject. Use ready-made glitter elements like stars and letters to make the page shine. Add embossed die-cuts for texture and top those off with glitter as well. For even more shimmer, add colorful rhinestone gems that look like dazzling holiday lights.

by Brenda Neuberger

Supplies: Cardstock; letters, glitter stars (Making Memories); chipboard, patterned paper, ribbon (Rusty Pickle); embossing powder (Jo-Ann Essentials); glitter glue (Ranger); gems (Kaiser Craft); transparency (My Mind's Eye); Misc: ink

Let the words flow

It just doesn't get more unique than holiday bingo. But even if you're scrapping a typical holiday event, you can take a lesson from Marci to make your page special. When telling your story, let the words flow and give yourself permission to make a two-page layout even with only one or two photos. Also, let creative design elements take center stage. Marci created a bingo border using leftover number rub-ons and stickers. Not only does this enhance the layout's theme, but it's also a great idea for using leftover supplies.

by Marci Lambert

Supplies: Cardstock; patterned paper (7Gypsies, Daisy D's); rub-ons (7Gypsies, Making Memories); stickers (7Gypsies); stamps (PSX, StampCraft, EK Success, Fontwerks); ribbon (Wright's); Misc: ink, punches

Bring it to life

Kimber's Christmas layout is a great example of how to bring any seasonal layout to life. Just shake things up and turn your elements—photos, patterned paper, journaling, title—on an angle. It offers a fresh twist on any theme, and it's great for scrapping Christmas, which is a task that can become mundane after many years. Another great idea on this layout is the addition of a quote from Kimber's son, which draws us into the moment. Employ this technique on a layout as another way to bring a page to life.

by Kimber McGray

Supplies: Cardstock (Core'dinations); patterned paper, die-cuts (Jillibean Soup); alphas (American Crafts, Doodlebug); Misc: punch

oh christmas tea

oh christmas tea

Every year, to kick off the Christmas season, the women of St. John's hold their annual Christmas Tea. The tables are decorated extravagantly, and we all try to outdo each other. It's a bit of friendly competition where everyone wins. Merry Christmas!

photos dec. '07

Use holiday songs

Making a holiday layout extra-special doesn't take much—just a few words will do. Janet's layout displays a beautiful collection of photos from an annual church Christmas tea. It also features a title that plays on words from the song "Oh Christmas Tree." Try this simple technique when adding a title to your own holiday layout. Turn to the Internet to search for titles and lyrics that might spark some creativity.

by Janet Ohlson

Supplies: Papers by Katie Pertiet and Anna Aspnes (Designer Digitals); template by Anna Aspnes (Designer Digitals); Misc: Suede and Porcelain fonts

This Christmas was a wonderful season, both for the kids and for me. The children were happy to be spoiled rotten, but the high point for me was finally seeing my whole family healthy. Papa's heart was beating strong, Great-Grandma Mackenzie was out of the hospital, Allen's allergies were under control, and no one was suffering. I know that our good health won't last forever, but this small window of delight will live eternally in my heart.

~2007

Strip your photos

The holidays are hectic enough, so keep layouts simple. But even on a simple page, you can still kick it up. Trimming your photos into strips, as Sabrina did, will allow you to maximize the number of photos on your layout, and it provides a fresh take on the typical. This is one of the simplest ways to tackle all those holiday photos. Also try creating this layout as a two-page version with the photo strip continuing onto a second page.

by Sabrina Ropp

Supplies: Cardstock; patterned paper, chipboard (BasicGrey); felt (QuickKutz); brads (Oriental Trading Company, Making Memories); Misc: ink

At our house the 1st thing we open on Christmas morning is our Stockings. Everything in them is wrapped so it takes a few minutes to get to each goodie.

Stockings

JOY

Christmas Morning 12/07

Tie it together

Christmas traditions vary from house to house. Kimber's family spends Christmas morning opening stocking presents, and this layout captures her daughter caught up in the excitement. Since nothing says Christmas more than a package, why not wrap up your own layout? Just add some trim to the background and tie on a journaling tag, as Kimber did. It's an easy way to turn your layout into something special.

by Kimber McGray

Supplies: Patterned paper, metal, ribbon (We R Memory Keepers); alphas (American Crafts); tag (Bazzill); Misc: glitter

This was Grandma's year to be spoiled. With the help of Brad, Grandpa's personal shopper, Grandma received her first digital camera and MP3 player. She couldn't have been more excited about her new gadgets. Now her daily walks would be filled with song. She could take as many photos of her grandchildren and only develop her favorites. It was in deed a very merry hi-tech Christmas. 12/2005

Go graphic

Our scrapbooks are filled with tons of photos showing off what our children get every year for Christmas, but often the rest of the family gets neglected. Several years ago Summer's mother-in-law received some cool electronic gadgets, which Summer documented on this layout. Try Summer's simple, no-fail approach for creating quick holiday layouts. Base your layout off a 3 × 3 grid pattern; mix photos and coordinating patterned paper and set them on a neutral background. The graphic formula is easily translated into a two-page layout, and it works as a template for tons of layout themes.

by Summer Fullerton

Supplies: Cardstock; patterned paper, stickers (October Afternoon); brads (BasicGrey); chipboard (Heidi Grace); die-cuts (Doodlebug); gems (Kaisercraft)

christmas in Summer

Traditional Christmas television and advertisements are full of snowflakes and singing carols on a cold winter night. Of course the reality is very different here. For me Christmas is truly in the air when I see the bursting Crimson colour of the Pohutukawa tree around the beach coastlines, like an invitation to come play underneath their large branches. Christmas Eve arrives and the kids have trouble falling asleep with it being light until after 9pm at night. Christmas lunch is generally a cold lunch or BBQ. Cold cream desserts, riding bikes down the street with other kids and their new bikes, water fights or falling asleep in the sun is always on the menu.

There is always time to play with new toys as most people pack up and take annual holidays to a favourite place or beach just after the big day. Christmas is the start of a long hot summer. Not a snowflake in sight!

Record it no matter what

Typically, Christmas layouts feature kids all bundled up, but not for Nic Howard. Christmas doesn't look the same at her house in New Zealand. We were immediately drawn into this layout by the playful photos of her kids and great journaling. No matter where you celebrate the holidays—be it on the beach or on the slopes—there is always a memory to be recorded and celebrated in your scrapbooks.

by Nic Howard

Supplies: Cardstock; patterned paper (BasicGrey, My Mind's Eye); alphas (Heidi Swapp, Making Memories); transparency (My Mind's Eye); brads (Queen & Co.); rub-on (BasicGrey); Misc: border punch

Handwrite a background

Celebrate a non-traditional holiday with a non-traditional layout. Julie's eye-catching, artistic hand journaling draws us into the page. Not only does it capture her feelings from the day, but it also acts as the "patterned" paper. Using journaling as a background is a fresh technique that can work on many seasonal layouts. Not all of us consider ourselves great artists, so you can achieve a similar look using your computer and printer.

by Julie Fei-Fan Balzer

Supplies: Cardstock; watercolor (Winsor & Newton); Misc: ink

Share about yourself

Some layouts are more than they appear. At first glance, Julie's layout looks like an ordinary Hanukkah page. But given a closer look, it reveals the story behind the photos as Julie teaches us about her heritage. It's great to focus your scrapping on the product and the creative process—that's what all those goodies are for! But Julie's layout is a reminder to go deeper and share a part of ourselves through our art. A layout like this celebrates not only the holiday but heritage as well.

by Julie Fei-Fan Balzer

Supplies: Paper, elements (Balzer Designs); Misc: Kingthings Typewriter, Tiza and CK Ali's Handwriting fonts

It was a very special occasion when Mom turned 75! John & Rosanna hosted a beautiful dinner party to celebrate. The whole family came, including Veronica and baby Luke from Boston, and Karen flew in from St. Louis. We all ate and drank and had a wonderful time together. It was a very special and fun night. Mom is holding the card I made her in the photo. She loved it! 12/15/2007

Skip typical product

Birthdays are celebrated every year (whether we admit it or not), so it's hard to keep layout ideas fresh. Linda's mom celebrated her 75th birthday with friends and family in December, and Linda captured the event on this two-page layout. Linda skipped the typical birthday product (which would have clashed with the photos) and instead opted for a pretty page with simple, feminine accents. Linda also illustrates how cropping your photos to a small size helps you fit more on a page. Plus, placing a large focal point photo next to several smaller ones makes for a well-balanced design.

by Linda Sobolewski

Supplies: Cardstock; patterned paper, flower (Autumn Leaves); stickers (Autumn Leaves, American Crafts); Misc: buttons, brads

Winter Scrapping Checklist

- ☐ Hanukkah
- ☐ Holiday baking
- ☐ Holiday parties
- ☐ Holiday shopping and wrapping gifts
- ☐ Decorating the Christmas tree
- ☐ Christmas Eve/Day
- ☐ Kwanzaa
- ☐ New Year's celebrations and traditions
- ☐ New Year's resolutions
- ☐ Super Bowl Sunday
- ☐ Valentine's Day
- ☐ Mardi Gras
- ☐ First snowfall
- ☐ Outdoor activities like skiing, snowboarding, ice skating and sledding
- ☐ Snowball fights
- ☐ Winter getaway
- ☐ Winter sports such as basketball and hockey

List the year's events

The pages of the calendar have turned to the last; time to reflect on a year gone by. Liana uses this two-page spread to record the year's events in a creative way—using a month-by-month list outlining what she's thankful for. She also created a strip of photos, which mimics a time line of events, perfect for viewing a year in a flash. Scrapbooking the year at a glance is a great way to finish off an album. This formula can also be translated to other layouts when you might want to follow a time line of events, for example, for a baby's first year, the first year of college or an engagement.

by Liana Suwandi

Supplies: Patterned paper (BasicGrey); rub-ons (7Gypsies, BasicGrey); stickers (Creative Imaginations); brads (Making Memories); Misc: ink

We had a blast with our friends bringing in 2003. I didn't know it would be the ONLY Yr. we would celebrate together. so i cherish that night even more.

2003

hello new

Start the year off right

Each year begins the same: No matter where you are, the clock changes and a new year begins. Where were you at the start of the year? Kim Hughes rang in 2003 with friends, and a single photo from the evening left her with a cherished memory she recorded on this page. Accents like clocks and numbered die-cut paper help reinforce the New Year's theme. And take a closer look at the photo—notice that it's panoramic, fitting perfectly across the page, the empty space a landing spot for the title and journaling. Altogether, it's a new perspective for a new year.

by Kim Hughes

Supplies: Cardstock (Core'dinations, KI Memories); acrylic (Heidi Swapp); patterned paper (BasicGrey); stickers (American Crafts, Around the Block); rhinestones (Me & My Big Ideas)

Record your goals

Of course, most of our scrapbooking time is spent getting memories of family and friends recorded on layouts. How about trying something new this year? Create a layout about yourself! And what better opportunity than the start of a new year to reflect? Recording your goals or resolutions for the year is a great way to share a little something about yourself. Try a simple journaling prompt like Summer used ("I will …") and see where your thoughts take you.

by Summer Ford

Supplies: Cardstock; patterned paper (Tinkering Ink); chipboard (The Paper Studio); rub-ons (BasicGrey, Tinkering Ink); brads (Pebbles Inc., Making Memories); Misc: acrylic paint, punch

Record a single resolution

Like Summer, Laura opted to scrap her goals for the year on this New Year's layout. But she chose to focus on just one goal—getting a clean house. So she snapped a few photos to record the start of her New Year's goal. Her use of curved journaling lines provides a unique and whimsical look for the layout, and it complements the feel of the busy, messy photos.

by Laura O'Donnell

Supplies: Cardstock; stamps (Technique Tuesday); stickers (Making Memories); Misc: ink

As I sit and write this, the windchill is -11. In the midst of icy roads, slush and below zero temperatures, I see beauty. There is nothing more refreshing than a new blanket of snow. I love the contrast of the trees against crisp, white snow. I love rosy, winter cheeks on children's faces. Some people see winter as treacherous, cold and annoying. I see the magic it brings out in nature and my children.

winter magic

Crack the background

We love Lisa's glass-half-full approach to remembering the cold days of winter. One day, she sat back and recorded all she observed, from the blustery temperatures to the icy roads. Lisa discovered by accident that you can create a cracked ice look using heated embossing powder. Her reflective journaling and creative snowflake techniques make this layout truly unique.

By Lisa Dorsey

Supplies: Cardstock; pattern papers (K&Co., KI Memories, Creative Imaginations); alphas (K&Co.); foam snowflakes (Creative Hands); stamp (Purple Onion); buttons (Creative Imaginations); Misc: glitter

Make an Icy Background

WHAT YOU'LL NEED

cardstock (or heavy-duty patterned paper), watermark ink, thick embossing powder, heat gun, glitter, rubber stamp

1 Stamp watermark ink onto a small portion of the background cardstock.

2 Shake a generous amount of thick embossing powder onto the inked area. Pour excess powder back into the container.

3 Using a heat gun, heat the powder until it's completely melted. You can tell it's completely melted when there are no more granules and the surface has a shiny appearance. Repeat steps 1–3 over the same area to create a thick layer. You might notice that the cardstock buckles under the melted powder—that's okay, it's supposed to!

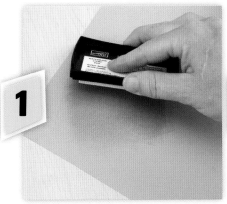

4 Pour a bit of glitter onto a scrap piece of paper. Ink the rubber stamp with watermark ink. Stamp into the glitter. Tap off the excess glitter.

5 Heat up the melted embossing power on your background in the area that you want to stamp. Quickly stamp into the melted powder.

6 Repeat steps 1-5 to fill the remainder of the background, if desired. Let the melted powder cool for about 10 minutes. (If you are short on time, stick the project in the refrigerator.) Once the powder cools, flatten the cardstock to create cracks in the melted powder.

Try out white on white

You might think that setting snow photos on top of a white background is a no-no. It's true that getting snow photos to pop on a layout requires some finesse, but using white on white is a modern approach to layout design. To ensure that snow photos stand out, simply frame your photos in a bright color as Mary did with outlines in orange. Mary added her photo frame digitally, but you can easily re-create the look on a traditional layout using colored cardstock, ink or paint.

by Mary Rogers

Supplies: Paper by Jesse Edwards and Lynn Grieiveson (Designer Digitals); ledger grids by Katie Pertiet (Designer Digitals); simple torn edges, fruehling texture brushes by Anna Aspnes (Designer Digitals); swirl brush work by Kellie Mize (Designer Digitals); snowflakes (Amanda Roberts)

Scrap the bad with the good

Not every winter trip has a happy ending—just ask Summer about her "Misadventure" on the ski slopes. But that doesn't mean the layout can't be lighthearted and cheery, especially if the photos are colorful and bright. This layout reminds us to scrapbook every story, no matter the outcome. Summer took a light approach to her journaling, infusing it with a touch a humor.

by Summer Ford

Supplies: Cardstock; patterned paper (Scenic Route); chipboard (The Paper Studio, All My Memories, American Crafts, Scenic Route); stamp, staples (Making Memories); label (Dymo); brads (The Paper Studio); ribbon (Offray); Misc: ink, acrylic paint

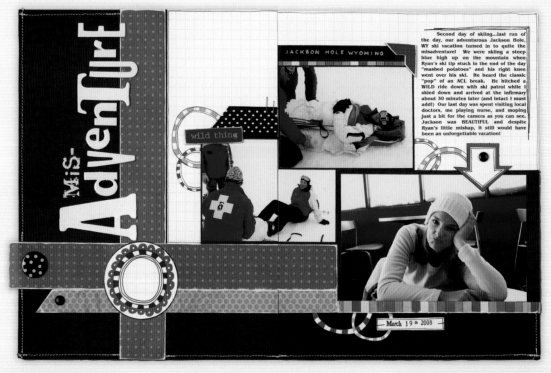

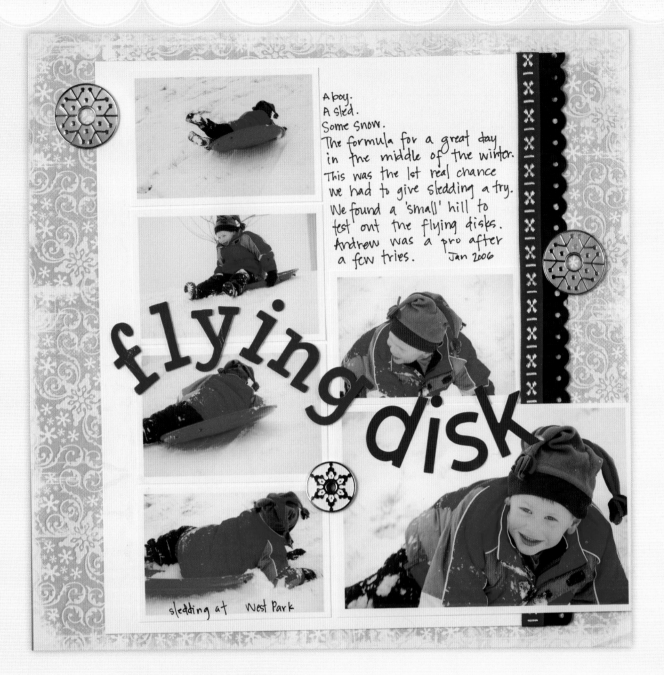

A boy.
A sled.
Some snow.
The formula for a great day in the middle of the winter. This was the 1st real chance we had to give sledding a try. We found a 'small' hill to test out the flying disks. Andrew was a pro after a few tries.   Jan 2006

flying disk

sledding at West Park

Liven up the title

If you are fortunate enough (or unlucky enough, depending on your perspective) to live where it snows, you have probably amassed a collection of snow-related photos from over the years. With all that white, snow photos tend to look rather similar, making for layouts that become stale over time. One way to keep a page exciting is to employ a creative title technique. Kimber's wavy title adds movement to the page, making it come alive. Lively titles are also a great fit for photos, like Kimber's, showing lots of fun activity.

by Kimber McGray

Supplies: Cardstock; patterned paper, metal, ribbon (We R Memory Keepers); alphas (American Crafts, Luxe Designs); Misc: punch

Reinforce the theme

Stop and take note of the changes in the seasons to find different ways to scrap the year. With ice and snow, winter brings a whole new array of glorious photo opportunities. Kimber stepped outside and captured the essence of a Midwest winter. Ice-coated branches make for spectacular photos, and neutral patterned papers enhance the scenery. Reinforce an icy theme on your layouts by adding transparent accents.

by Kimber McGray

Supplies: Patterned paper (Pink Paislee); alphas (Heidi Swapp, American Crafts); brads (We R Memory Keepers); acrylic (Heidi Swapp); Misc: ink

Take advantage of the season

The cold weather brings us inside for the season so take advantage of the extra time on your hands and get scrapbooking. Winter is the perfect time of year to hole up with your scrapbook supplies and tackle lots of new projects. And 'tis the season for giving—make a mini-album or calendar for a family member or get crafty with your kids and make homemade holiday decorations.

Add die-cut paper

People aren't the only ones who enjoy playing in the snow. Don't forget to scrapbook the four-legged friends in your life. Beth caught her dog's first experience in the snow on film and created this adorable layout. Follow Beth's lead by accenting winter-themed layouts with die-cut paper; it's reminiscent of snowflakes, and comes in many patterns and colors to match any of your photos.

by Beth Warren

Supplies: Cardstock; patterned paper (Fancy Pants); die-cut (KI Memories); chipboard, acrylic (Heidi Swapp)

Switch to happy hues

Don't let the winter doldrums keep you from creating cheery pages in warm colors. In a sea of white and icy blue, warm hues will pop. Barbara's layout about her birdhouse takes us straight outdoors and has us wishing for spring. Taking a cue from her photos, Barbara applied bright orange and blue patterned paper on the digital layout, adding pretty details like ribbon and scallops. Follow Barbara's lead and highlight your layout with a color pulled from your photos.

by Barbara Albrecht

Supplies: Spring Breeze Kit by Michelle Shefveland (Scrapper's Guide); Midnight Magic Kit by Michaela Ferkul (Microferk Designs); photo frames by Paislee Press (OScraps); scallop cutting template (Seebee's Freebies); flower by Linda Sattgast (Scrapper's Guide); Misc: travel album kit

Surprise the viewer

Express love in your scrapbook pages by documenting romance. Romantic layouts don't have to be red, pink and packed with hearts and flowers. In fact, going in another direction as Kathie did will keep winter layouts fresh. Kathie also added a gatefold element, which reveals the journaling and more photos, and provides something unexpected. On your own seasonal layout, add a surprise element—like a pocket or a folding card—to engage the viewer and provide a place for lots of words and extra photos.

by Kathie Davis

Supplies: Cardstock; patterned paper (Rusty Pickle, My Mind's Eye, Die Cuts With A View); chipboard (Rusty Pickle, Grafix, Heidi Swapp); rub-ons (Rusty Pickle); spray paint (Krylon); magnet (Magnum)

Great Wolf Lodge absolutely blew you away! You described it as "the best place I have ever been, Mom!" From the moment you arrived you began plotting your return.

~January, 2008~

GREAT WOLF LODGE

Make photos be square

Vacations don't always happen during the summertime. To escape the winter blues, Sarah and her family went to the Great Wolf Lodge. Sarah squeezed in lots of fun-filled photos by cropping most of them to the same square size, leaving just one large photo to pop as the focal point. The symmetry of the design provides calm against the busyness of the photos, and the cardstock background lends balance. For a unique title treatment great for a wintry layouts, stamp letters using white acrylic paint like Sarah did.

by Sarah Hodgkinson

Supplies: Cardstock; patterned paper (SEI, Scenic Route); overlay (Hambly); stamps (Gel-a-tins, K&Co.); brads (Making Memories); Misc: ink, acrylic paint

Hand draw details

For sports fans, winter means enjoying basketball season. Emily sent us this layout recording her daughter's second season playing the sport. This layout pairs five small photos with whimsical touches like a hand-cut scalloped border and hand-drawn journaling strips. Emily shows it doesn't take much to make seasonal layouts fun and different. So give all those fancy tools a rest and devote some time to pen and ink. Hand-drawn details will provide a fresh look and energetic feel perfect for action-oriented pages.

by Emily Pitts

Supplies: Cardstock; brad (American Crafts); alphas (Doodlebug Designs); metal tag (Avery); Misc: thread

Fashion easy scallop borders

WHAT YOU'LL NEED

two papers (one for border and one other); adhesive; pencil and scissors, circle punches or scallop border punch

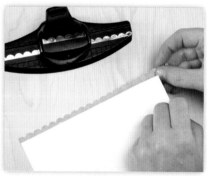

Easy: Hand Drawn
Layer the paper for the scallop border behind your other piece of paper. The border should be about 1" (3cm) wide. In pencil, draw a scallop border around the page. Imperfections are OK—that's the whole idea! Cut out the border.

Easier: Circle Punch
Punch circles from the border paper. For a more whimsical look, use different punch sizes. Then attach them behind the other paper, adhering the bottom half to the paper and allowing the top half to peek up from behind.

Easiest: Border Punch
Using a scallop border punch, punch a border in the border paper. The border should be as long as the other paper's edge. Attach the straight edge of the border to the back edge of the top sheet of paper.

Embrace photo flaws

With all that action, obtaining good sports photos can be difficult, especially indoors with poor lighting. Emily encountered this hiccup when her daughter played volleyball in middle school. But Emily didn't let that get in the way of making a great seasonal page. Turning the blurry photos to black and white and printing them small helped Emily take the emphasis off the poor quality. Punching circles out of the photos and patterned paper to create a grid design also hides the flaws by putting the "focus" on an interesting design.

by Emily Pitts

Supplies: Cardstock; patterned paper (October Afternoon, Scenic Route); alphas (BasicGrey); Misc: acrylic paint, ink

Make photos move

Sherry spends each winter watching her son play ice hockey. She created this layout to show off her son's winning efforts. Her layout stands out from the pack with the placement of photos that creates movement on the page. Notice how the photos get progressively larger—from the small photo in the center to the larger photo outside—in a spiral motion. It almost looks as if they are about to burst off the page. The page also shines with glittery stars. Altogether it's a winning design for a winning theme.

by Sherry Steveson

Supplies: Patterned paper (BasicGrey); alphas (Luxe Designs, Making Memories, American Crafts); chipboard shapes (Li'l Davis, Rusty Pickle); acrylic (Hambly); rub-on (Heidi Swapp); Misc: glitter

Celebrating Australia Day with Daniel. Steve, Paul & Susie - good friends, a bbq and beautiful weather - just perfect :) january 26 2007

Australia Day

Balance a lot on a page

The date may say January, but this certainly isn't a winter layout! Kim's page tells us about Australia Day, which is celebrated in Australia every January 26. Aside from the lack of snow, what makes this winter layout unusual is that Kim managed to balance seven photos, a title and journaling on a one-page layout. To re-create this look on your own page, start with a 4" × 6" (10cm × 15cm) photo as the center of the design. Cut the remaining photos to a smaller size and place them around the focal photo. Add journaling and a title in opposite corners and place simple accents throughout.

by Kim Arnold

Supplies: Patterned paper (Junkitz, BasicGrey); chipboard (Heidi Swapp)

Valentine's Day is such a sweet day to celebrate. Even for a little guy who is far from the days when he will have a 'Sweetheart' to go along with the festivities, you still get a lot of enjoyment out of the celebration of the day. The Valentine cards and treats you receive every year from your preschool classmates sure help to get you excited. And sharing any Valentine chocolates that may be around the house certainly help to get you into the spirit. But not much beats the joy of a great Valentine's Day as finding a big box left for you at our door from a certain someone who thinks especially of you on each and every Valentine's Day. Yes, a package of love...and chocolates...and cash ...sure does help to put one little guy in the Valentine spirit in one BIG way. Your Grammo's love for you is bigger than any present she could buy.

February 2008

Make it simply sweet

Linda's son returned home from school on Valentine's Day to a wonderful surprise—a package from his grandma. A few snapshots later and this layout was born. Of course Valentine's Day layouts require a bit of love, but you can avoid going completely ooey-gooey. Take cues from Linda's page, which is set with a plain kraft cardstock background. A sophisticated red pattern brings out the color in the photos, while the bright blue title cools it down a bit. Linda couldn't resist adding hearts to the page, but a button-topped transparency and hand-stitched felt make the page more simply sweet than saccharine.

by Linda Harrison

Supplies: Cardstock; patterned paper (Scenic Route); alphas (BasicGrey, Scenic Route); scallops (Paper Source); buttons, ribbon (SEI); sheers (Maya Road); stickers (Scrapworks, Little Yellow Bicycle); felt (Fancy Pants); floss (DMC); metal (SEI, Making Memories); chipboard (Scenic Route)

Layout Sketches

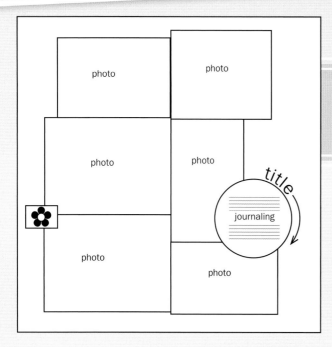

Pike Place Market
By Marie Lottermoser
Page 49

Hurricane Ready
By Linda Harrison
Page 65

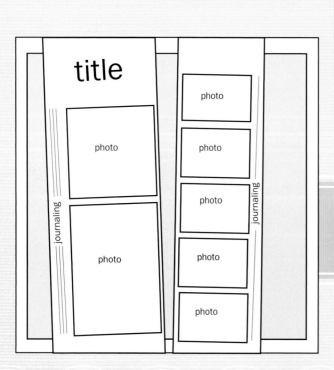

I Spy
By Summer Fullerton
Page 45

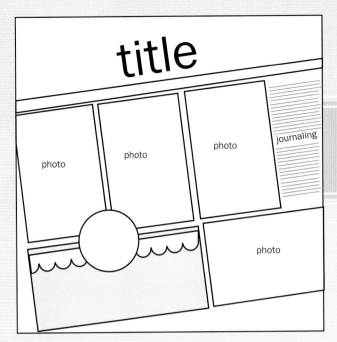

Santa Was Here
By Kimber McGray
Page 93

Day Trip to Cobh
By Paula Gilarde
Page 42

'09 Resolutions
By Summer Ford
Page 103

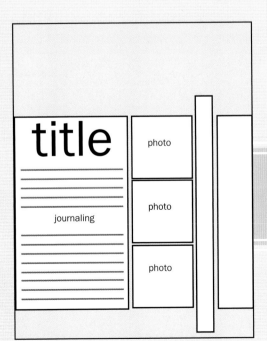

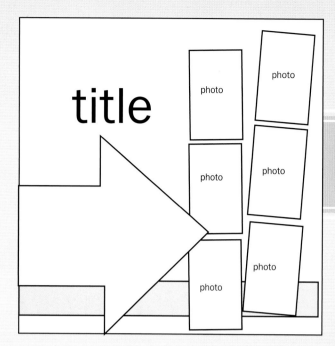

Road Trip
By Kim Moreno
Page 48

title

photo
photo
photo
photo
photo
photo

journaling

photo

photo

photo

photo
photo

photo
photo

photo
photo

photo
photo

title

patterned paper

Great Wolf Lodge
By Sarah Hodgkinson
Page 111

photo

photo

photo

journaling

title

journaling

photo

photo

Gorden's Garden
By Tricia Gorden
Page 57

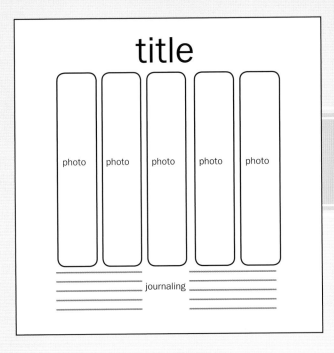

title

photo · photo · photo · photo · photo

journaling

Happy St. Patrick's Day
By Katrina Kennedy
Page 15

Play Hard
By Angie Hagist
Page 39

title

photo

photo

journaling

Do Not Disturb
By Summer Fullerton
Page 73

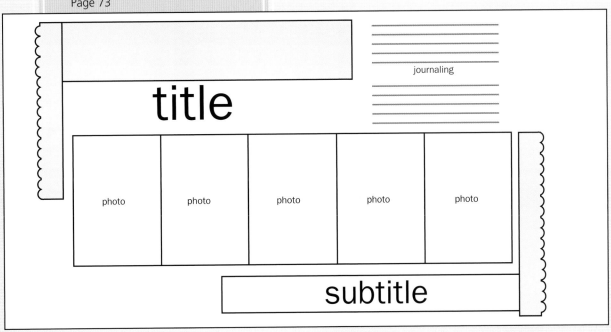

title

journaling

photo · photo · photo · photo · photo

subtitle

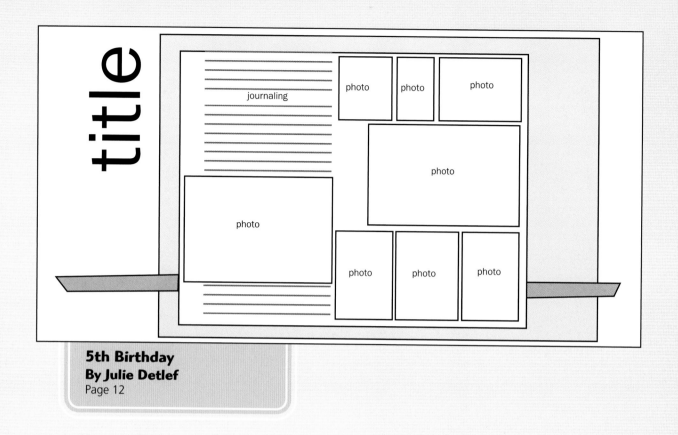

5th Birthday
By Julie Detlef
Page 12

The Zoo
By Leigh Penner
Page 22

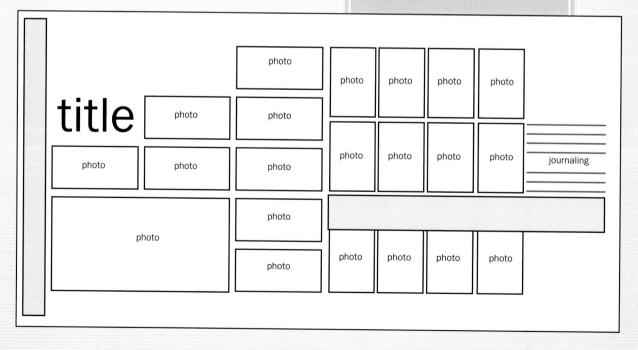

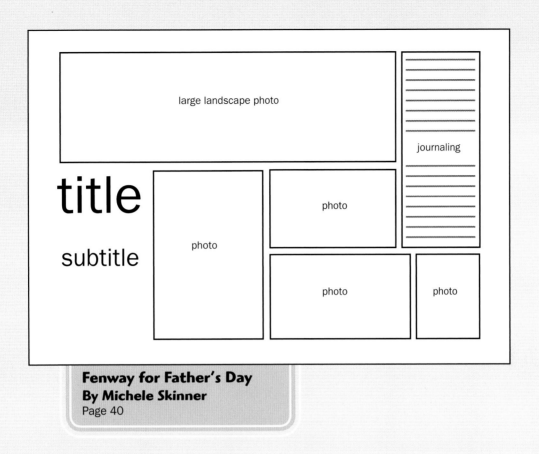

Fenway for Father's Day
By Michele Skinner
Page 40

Up on His Hill
By Shannon Taylor
Page 74

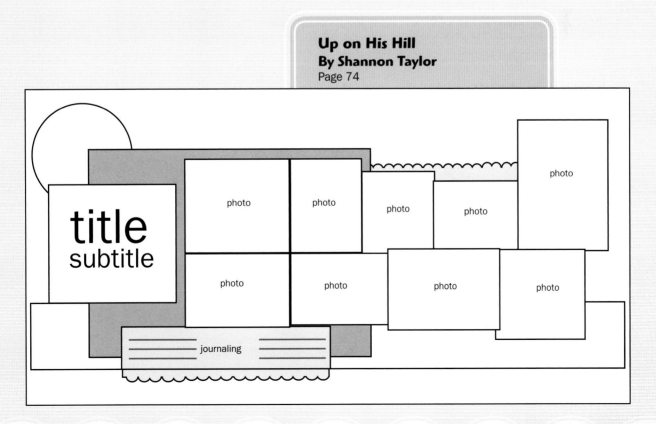

Yearly Scrapping Checklist

Use this handy-dandy checklist to keep on top of scrapping the events that pop up throughout the year.

Spring

- [ ] Cinco de Mayo
- [ ] A day at the park
- [ ] Easter or Passover
- [ ] First blooms of the season
- [ ] Gardening
- [ ] March Madness
- [ ] Memorial Day
- [ ] Mother's Day
- [ ] Outdoor parties
- [ ] Prom
- [ ] Spring break
- [ ] Spring cleaning
- [ ] St. Patrick's Day
- [ ] Spring sports
- [ ] Trip to the farmer's market

Summer

- [ ] Berry picking
- [ ] Bike riding
- [ ] Camping
- [ ] Family reunions
- [ ] Father's Day
- [ ] Fourth of July
- [ ] Graduation
- [ ] Last day of school
- [ ] Local festivals and fairs
- [ ] Outdoor activities likes fishing and hiking
- [ ] Picnics and cookouts
- [ ] Summer festivals
- [ ] Summer sports such as golf, swimming or tennis
- [ ] Vacations and road trips
- [ ] Water activities

Fall

- [ ] Apple picking
- [ ] Back to school
- [ ] Carving pumpkins
- [ ] Enjoying fall treats like apple cider, pumpkin pie and caramel apples
- [ ] Fall leaves
- [ ] Fall sports such as football, soccer, cheerleading
- [ ] Halloween activities
- [ ] Harvest parties
- [ ] Hayrides
- [ ] Homecoming festivities
- [ ] Labor Day
- [ ] Planting bulbs
- [ ] Thanksgiving
- [ ] Veteran's Day
- [ ] Visit to the pumpkin patch

Winter

- [ ] Christmas Eve/Day
- [ ] Decorating the Christmas tree
- [ ] First snowfall
- [ ] Hanukkah
- [ ] Holiday baking
- [ ] Holiday parties
- [ ] Holiday shopping
- [ ] Kwanzaa
- [ ] Mardi Gras
- [ ] New Year's celebrations
- [ ] Outdoor activities like skiing or snowboarding
- [ ] Sledding
- [ ] Snowball fights
- [ ] Super Bowl Sunday
- [ ] Valentine's Day
- [ ] Winter getaway
- [ ] Winter sports such as basketball or hockey
- [ ] Wrapping gifts

Anytime

- [ ] Anniversary
- [ ] Baptism/christening
- [ ] Birth/adoption
- [ ] Birthdays
- [ ] Girl/Boy Scout activities
- [ ] First car/driver's license
- [ ] New house
- [ ] Wedding

Calendar Template

Copy this template each month and use it to help you plan out a month's worth of scrapping activities.

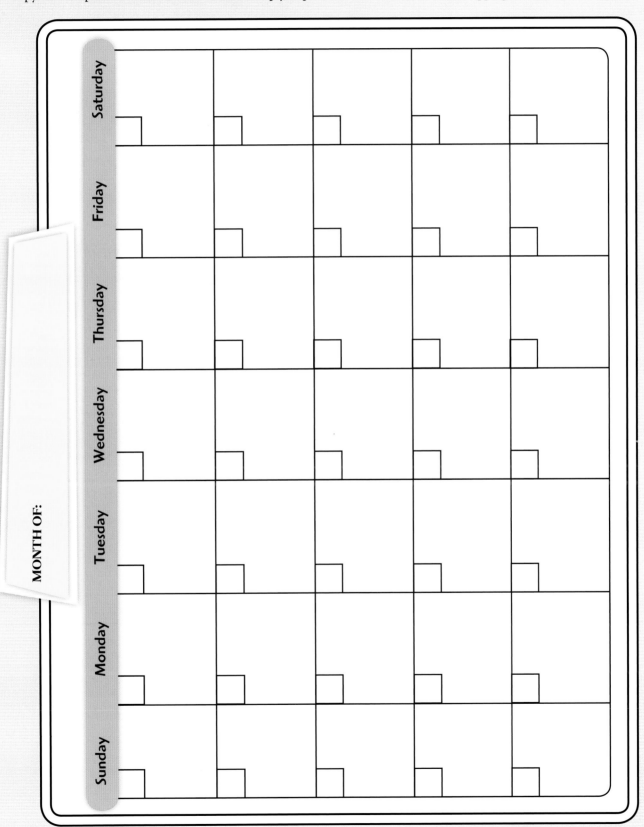

MONTH OF:

Sunday | Monday | Tuesday | Wednesday | Thursday | Friday | Saturday

Source Guide

The following companies manufacture products featured in this book. Please check your local retailers to find these materials, or go to a company's Web site for the latest product. In addition, we have made every attempt to properly credit the items mentioned in this book. We apologize to any company that we have listed incorrectly, and we would appreciate hearing from you.

7gypsies
(877) 749-7797
www.sevengypsies.com

A2Z Essentials
Info not available

Adornit/Carolee's Creations
(435) 563-1100
www.adornit.com

All My Memories
(904) 482-0092
www.allmymemories.com

American Crafts
(801) 737-9197
www.americancrafts.com

Around The Block
(801) 593-1946
www.aroundtheblock
products.com

Autumn Leaves
(800) 727-2727
www.autumnleaves.com

Avery Dennison Corporation
(800) 462-8379
www.avery.com

Balzer Designs
www.balzardesigns.
typepad.com

BasicGrey
(801) 544-1116
www.basicgrey.com

Bazzill Basics Paper
(800) 560-1610
www.bazzillbasics.com

Beaux Regards
No info available

Berwick Offray, LLC
(800) 237-9425
www.offray.com

BoBunny Press
(801) 771-4010
www.bobunny.com

Carolee's Creations
—see Adornit

Chatterbox, Inc.
(877) 749-7797
www.chatterboxinc.com

Cloud 9 Design
(866) 348-5661
cloud9design.wordpress.com

Coats & Clark
(800) 648-1479
www.coatsandclark.com

Cocoa Daisy
www.cocoadaisy.com

Collage Press
(435) 676-2039
www.collagepress.com

Contact Brand
www.contactbrand.com

Core'dinations
www.coredinations.com

Cosmo Cricket
(800) 852-8810
www.cosmocricket.com

Crate Paper
(801) 798-8996
www.cratepaper.com

Creative Hands
www.creativehands.com

Creative Imaginations
(800) 942-6487
www.cigift.com

Creative Impressions
(719) 596-4860
www.creativeimpressions.com

Daisy D's Paper Company
(888) 601-8955
www.daisydspaper.com

Darice, Inc.
(866) 432-7423
www.darice.com

Dèjá Views/C-Thru Ruler
(800) 243-0303
www.dejaviews.com

Designer Digitals
www.designerdigitals.com

Die Cuts With A View
(801) 224-6766
www.diecutswithaview.com

Digital Design Essentials
www.digitaldesignessentials.
com

DMC Corp.
(973) 589-0606
www.dmc-usa.com

Doodlebug Design Inc.
(877) 800-9190
www.doodlebug.ws

Dream Street Papers
(480) 275-9736
www.dreamstreetpapers.com

Dreaming in Pixels
www.dreaminginpixels.com

Dress It Up/Jesse James & Co., Inc.
www.dressitup.com

Dymo
(800) 426-7827
www.dymo.com

EK Success, Ltd.
www.eksuccess.com

Fancy Pants Designs, LLC
(801) 779-3212
www.fancypantsdesigns.com

Fontwerks
(604) 942-3105
www.fontwerks.com

GCD Studios
www.gcdstudios.com

Gel-a-Tins
(800) 393-2151
www.gelatinstamps.com

Glitz Design
(866) 356-6131
www.glitzitnow.com

Hambly Screen Prints
(800) 707-0977
www.hamblyscreenprints.com

Heidi Grace Designs, Inc.
Info not available

Heidi Swapp/Advantus Corporation
(904) 482-0092
www.heidiswapp.com

Hero Arts Rubber Stamps, Inc.
(800) 822-4376
www.heroarts.com

Imagination Project, Inc.—no longer in business

Imaginisce
(801) 908-8111
www.imaginisce.com

Inque Boutique Inc.
www.inqueboutique.com

Jenni Bowlin
www.jennibowlin.com

Jillibean Soup
www.jillibean-soup.com

Jo-Ann Stores
www.joann.com

Junkitz
—no longer in business

K&Company
(800) 794-5866
www.kandcompany.com

Kaisercraft
www.kaisercraft.net

Karen Foster Design
(801) 451-9779
www.karenfosterdesign.com

KI Memories
(972) 243-5595
www.kimemories.com

Krylon
(800) 457-9566
www.krylon.com

Li'l Davis Designs
(480) 223-0080
www.lildavisdesigns.com

Little Dreamer Designs
www.littledreamerdesigns.com

Little Yellow Bicycle
—see Dèjá Views

Loew-Cornell, Inc.
www.loew-cornell.com

LuminArte (formerly
Angelwing Enterprises)
(866) 229-1544
www.luminarteinc.com

Luxe Designs
(972) 573-2120
www.luxedesigns.com

Magic Mesh
(651) 345-6374
www.magicmesh.com

Making Memories
(801) 294-0430
www.makingmemories.com

Martha Stewart Crafts
www.marthastewartcrafts.com

May Arts
www.mayarts.com

Maya Road, LLC
(877) 427-7764
www.mayaroad.com

Me & My Big Ideas
(949) 583-2065
www.meandmybigideas.com

Michaels Arts & Crafts
www.michaels.com

Microferk Designs
www.microferkdesigns.
blogspot.com

Mustard Moon
(763) 493-5157
www.mustardmoon.com

My Mind's Eye, Inc.
(800) 665-5116
www.mymindseye.com

Narratives

Natalie Malan

October Afternoon
www.octoberafternoon.com

Offray
—see Berwick Offray, LLC

Oriental Trading Company
www.orientaltrading.com

Oscraps
www.oscraps.com

Pageframe Designs
www.scrapbookframe.com

Paper Source
(888) 727-3711
www.paper-source.com

Paper Studio
(480) 557-5700
www.paperstudio.com

Pebbles Inc.
(800) 438-8153
www.pebblesinc.com

Piggy Tales
(702) 755-8600
www.piggytales.com

Pink Paislee
(816) 729-6124
www.pinkpaislee.com

Plaid Enterprises, Inc.
(800) 842-4197
www.plaidonline.com

Prima Marketing, Inc.
(909) 627-5532
www.primamarketinginc.com

Provo Craft
(800) 937-7686
www.provocraft.com

PSX Design
www.sierra-enterprises.
com/psxmain.html

Purple Onion Designs
www.purpleoniondesigns.com

Purple Tulip Designs
www.purpletulipdesigns.
blogspot.com

Queen & Co.
(858) 613-7858
www.queenandcompany.com

QuicKutz, Inc.
(888) 702-1146
www.quickutz.com

Ranger Industries, Inc.
www.rangerink.com

Rusty Pickle
(801) 746-1045
www.rustypickle.com

Sandylion Sticker Designs
(800) 387-4215
www.sandylion.com

Sassafras Lass
(801) 269-1331
www.sassafraslass.com

Scenic Route Paper Co.
(801) 653-1319
www.scenicroutepaper.com

Scrap Girls
(866) 598-3444
www.scrapgirls.com

Scrapper's Guide
www.scrappersguide.com

Scrappin' Sports & More
www.scrappinsports.com

Scrapworks, LLC
(801) 363-1010
www.scrapworks.com

SEI, Inc.
(800) 333-3279
www.shopsei.com

Shabby Princess
www.shabbyprincess.com

Sonburn, Inc.
(800) 436-4919
www.sonburn.com

Stampin' Up!
(800) 782-6787
www.stampinup.com

Staples, Inc.
www.staples.com

**Stewart Superior
Corporation**
(800) 558-2875
www.stewartsuperior.com

Tattered Angels
www.mytatteredangels.com

Technique Tuesday, LLC
(503) 644-4073
www.techniquetuesday.com

Teresa Collins
www.teresacollinsdesigns.com

Tim Holtz
www.timholtz.com

Tinkering Ink
(877) 727-2784
www.tinkeringink.com

Two Girlz Stuff
www.etsy.com/shop/
twogirlzstuff

Two Peas in a Bucket
(888) 896-7327
www.twopeasinabucket.com

**We R Memory Keepers,
Inc.**
(801) 539-5000
www.weronthenet.com

Winsor & Newton
www.winsornewton.com

**Wintech International
Corp.**
(800) 263-6043
www.wintechint.com

WorldWin Papers
(888) 843-6455
www.worldwinpapers.com

Wrights Ribbon Accents
(877) 597-4448
www.wrights.com

Zsiage, LLC
(718) 224-1976
www.zsiage.com

Index

About the Authors

KIMBER MCGRAY has been a crafter of some kind since she was a young child. She found her way into scrapbooking through a friend who pushed her for well over a year. Once she began to play with the papers and tools we all know and love, there was no turning back. She jumped in with two feet and has enjoyed every moment of it since. Over the last three years, Kimber has been fortunate to be published in all the major scrapbooking and card publications, and her first book, *Scrapbook Secrets,* was published by Memory Makers Books in 2009. Kimber was inducted into the 2007 Creating Keepsakes Hall of Fame. Kimber finds time to create the pages that fill her albums when she is not making memories with her husband and two children in her hometown of Carmel, Indiana.

SUMMER FULLERTON's creative journey began at a young age. She grew up surrounded by inspiration; her mother made dolls, jewelry, pottery and even designed wallpaper. It seemed natural for Summer to take a creative path in life as well. She received her first camera in 1976, and although it wasn't loaded with film until many years later, the seeds of artistry had been planted. Summer found herself drawn to photography and landed on the yearbook staffs in middle school, high school and college. After the birth of her first child, Summer discovered scrapbooking as we know it today and has been hooked ever since. In 2007 she was named to the Creating Keepsakes Hall of Fame and in 2009 she was a Memory Makers Master. Her published creations can be seen in *Creating Keepsakes, Scrapbooks Etc., Scrapbook Trends, Scrapbook & Cards Today, Paper Crafts* and *Cards.* Summer lives with her husband of 16 years and her two children in Tigard, Oregon.

Fill the year with great page ideas from these other Memory Makers Books

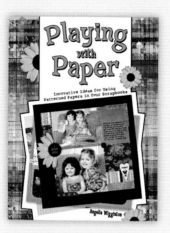

Outstanding Mini Albums
Jessica Acs

With inspiration, techniques and step-by-step projects for 50 fabulous albums, you'll see that showcasing your biggest memories is easy with adorable mini scrapbooks.

ISBN-13: 978-1-59963-032-8
ISBN-10: 1-59963-032-X
paperback
128 pages
Z2318

Playing with Paper
Angelia Wigginton

Lose your fear of patterned paper with ideas for mixing patterns in a wide variety of ways. Includes step-by-step instructions for creative but simple paper techniques.

ISBN-13: 978-1-59963-033-5
ISBN-10: 1-59963-033-8
paperback
128 pages
Z2390

The Scrapbook Embellishment Handbook
Sherry Steveson

Get fabulous ideas for using embellishments, from hot materials like acrylic to old standbys like stickers and stamps. With 51 illustrated techniques and more than 120 ideas for using all kinds of embellishments, this is your go-to guide for dressing up your layouts.

ISBN 13: 978-1-59963-035-9
ISBN 10: 1-59963-035-4
hardcover with enclosed spiral
144 pages
Z2495

Scrapbook Secrets
Kimber McGray

Get the scoop on 50 simple secrets that will help you scrap better, scrap faster and have fun along the way.

ISBN-13: 978-1-59963-034-2
ISBN-10: 1-59963-034-6
paperback
128 pages
Z2460

These books and other fine Memory Makers titles are available at your local scrapbook retailer, bookstore or from online suppliers, or visit our Web site at www.mycraftivitystore.com.